HELPING PARENTS OF DIAGNOSED, DISTRESSED, AND DIFFERENT CHILDREN

In *Helping Parents of Diagnosed, Distressed, and Different Children*, Eric Maisel provides clinicians with the tools they need to address the issues facing the parents of diagnosed children. In these pages, mental health professionals will find tips for using the right language to guide families through situations such as sibling bullying and parental divorce, as well as guidelines for thinking critically about children's mental health. Filled with hands-on resources including checklists and questionnaires, this valuable guide offers clinicians a set of strategies to help parents deal effectively with their child's distress, regardless of the source.

Eric Maisel, PhD, is a retired licensed psychotherapist, active creativity coach, and internationally respected expert in the field of mental health reform. He is the author of more than fifty books, writes the "Rethinking Mental Health" blog for *Psychology Today*, and serves as editor for parent resources at the website Mad in America, the world's largest critical psychiatry resource.

"Eric Maisel has written an important book in a time where almost every child has a diagnosis. As parents, it is up to us to educate ourselves that sometimes children exhibit behavior that is simply normal and needs to be worked through, and there is no need for a label to define our child."
— *Madisyn Taylor, cofounder, DailyOM and the author of Unmedicated: The Four Pillars of Natural Wellness*

"The medicalization of children's emotional and behavioral problems is a huge sociopolitical problem. It is supported by so many forces in our society that stopping, or even slowing it down, appears to be a huge uphill struggle. We truly need people like Eric Maisel who are willing to devote time, do the research, and expose the medical fallacy for what it is. Thank you, Eric, for your formidable job."
— *Ben Furman, psychiatrist and psychotherapist, founder of the Kids' Skills method*

HELPING PARENTS OF DIAGNOSED, DISTRESSED, AND DIFFERENT CHILDREN

A Guide for Professionals

Eric Maisel

NEW YORK AND LONDON

First published 2019
by Routledge
52 Vanderbilt Avenue, New York, NY 10017

and by Routledge
2 Park Square, Milton Park, Abingdon, Oxon OX14 4RN

Routledge is an imprint of the Taylor & Francis Group, an informa business

© 2019 Eric Maisel

The right of Eric Maisel to be identified as author of this work has been asserted by him in accordance with sections 77 and 78 of the Copyright, Designs and Patents Act 1988.

All rights reserved. No part of this book may be reprinted or reproduced or utilized in any form or by any electronic, mechanical, or other means, now known or hereafter invented, including photocopying and recording, or in any information storage or retrieval system, without permission in writing from the publishers.

Trademark notice: Product or corporate names may be trademarks or registered trademarks, and are used only for identification and explanation without intent to infringe.

Library of Congress Cataloging-in-Publication Data
A catalog record for this title has been requested

ISBN: 978-1-138-60292-2 (hbk)
ISBN: 978-1-138-60293-9 (pbk)
ISBN: 978-0-429-46102-6 (ebk)

Typeset in Joanna
by Swales & Willis, Exeter, Devon, UK

For Ann,
40 years into this adventure

CONTENTS

	Introduction: Your Client as Parent	1
1	Diagnosing or Labeling?	15
2	Deconstructing Attention Deficit Hyperactivity Disorder	30
3	Deconstructing Oppositional Defiant Disorder	44
4	Deconstructing Bipolar	57
5	Medication or Chemicals?	71
6	Thinking about Causes	85
7	Contemporary Approaches	102
8	Organizational Resources	117
9	Alternatives for "Serious Mental Illness"	133
10	What You Can Offer	151

| 11 | What Parents Can Do | 169 |
| 12 | Thirty-One Questions for Parents | 184 |

| Bibliography | 207 |
| Index | 208 |

INTRODUCTION
Your Client as Parent

Your client's mental and emotional wellbeing is significantly affected by how well or how poorly her child is doing.

If her child is a handful at home and at school, that reality may be the single most pressing problem she is currently facing. If her child is sad, moody, and uncommunicative, if her child is defiant and uncooperative, if her child seems to be sinking and failing, if her child is drinking heavily, all of that really matters.

On top of that very difficult reality, your client is also confronted by another painful reality: that the help offered her child by society is suspect. She will likely be told that her child has a "mental disorder" and she will also likely be told that her child ought to be medicated for that disorder. Now she has all that to face.

If you are a wise and humane helper, this is where you come in. Not only can you help her deal with her feelings, not only can you provide her with a safe place to air her thoughts and consider her options, but you can also serve as her guide through the minefields of the current dominant paradigm. That isn't to say that you will have all the answers, most of the answers, or even any good answers. You can't snap your fingers and turn her sad child into a happy child, her oppositional child into a cooperative child, or make sense for her of what her child's "voices" mean. What you can do, however, is sit with her, listen to her, and also educate her at least a little about those minefields. This means, of course, that you must educate yourself first.

A significant portion of this book is aimed at presenting you with a picture of the current situation from a "critical psychology" and "critical psychiatry" point of view. I'm sure you'll agree that it makes a tremendous difference—all the difference in the world—if a child is sad and discouraged and can be helped in non-medical ways to improve, or whether that child has a "mental disorder" called "childhood depression" that requires "psychiatric medication." Likewise, it makes a tremendous difference—all the difference in the world—if a child is anxious and fidgety because he is younger than his classmates and developmentally behind them or whether he has the "mental disorder" of "attention deficit hyperactivity disorder" that requires "psychiatric medication." I want to educate you on these debates, so that you can sit with your client as an informed helper.

This may be an especially hard time to be a parent. In addition to all of the other stresses put on parents, from paying bills to dealing with a child's toothaches, earaches, and teenage years, now a parent has to deal with—and quite likely protect herself from—the epidemic of "mental disorder" diagnosing (some would say labeling) that currently threatens millions of children and their parents. Indeed, many of your clients may find themselves in exactly this predicament and under this precise stress. What is going on?

We have certainly come a long way in our compassionate treatment of children. We no longer look at children as a workforce; we see them as having rights and deserving not to be abused; we believe that they have a right to be educated. Now, suddenly, in the course of just a handful of years, it looks as if we have taken a huge step backward. We are rushing down the road of turning every feature of childhood into a "symptom of a mental disorder" and turning every child into a "mental patient." Recently we have started down a new, dangerous road of "predicting mental disorders" in children and treating them prophylactically with chemicals called "medication" before they show any symptoms of a "mental disorder." Nowadays, children and their parents are besieged in these ways.

Holding Her Breath

Picture the following.

During World War II 60 million people died, more than 2.5% of the world's population. The Soviet Union alone lost between 18 and 24 million lives. Germany lost between 7 and 9 million, upwards of 10% of its population. Europe's Jewish population was reduced by between 5 and 6 million souls, or 55% of European Jewry. A country like Portugal lost "only" 50,000 of its citizens, but those 50,000 amounted to 10% of the Portuguese population.

Forget for a second who was in the right and who was in the wrong. Rather, imagine a German youth of 18, a Russian youth of 18, a British youth of 18, an American Jewish youth of 18, a French youth of 18, and a Japanese youth of 18. Think of the parents of each of these young men, parents, say, between 40 and 45 years old. Think of their grandparents. Think of their sisters, their younger brothers—think about everyone affected by that calamity. To say that the mental health of all of these people was merely "affected" by the experience of a world conflagration is to make a bad joke.

Affected, indeed! It may have been the defining, pressing, most important matter on their radar, completely altering their lives and producing year upon year of unbearable stress. The whole world's population was "motivated" in drastically new ways—and unmotivated as well. How motivated would you have been to open up your grocery store each morning if you had to sell to your Nazi oppressors? How motivated would you have been to get out of bed if your city was under siege? Now–think of a mother of one of those young soldiers and picture her as a client of yours.

Her son goes off to war, he has, say, a 20% or a 30% chance of dying, and for the years that he is away she is fundamentally not motivated at all, though of course she still drinks water when she is thirsty, plays the lottery in the hopes of a windfall, and shows up at work to receive her paycheck. She is still "motivated" in all the textbook ways—she gets to work, she buys lottery tickets, she drinks water, she has sex—but her reality is that she is holding her breath. If you ask her why she is having headaches, stomachaches, sleep problems, an inability to orgasm, and sudden crying fits, she may well tell you, "I am waiting for my son to come home." Should we really stand for a psychiatrist answering this with, "I have a pill for that mental disorder"? We should not.

A wise helper would reply simply and humanely: "I know." He or she would say to her,

> I understand. I know that you are holding your breath and I know why you are holding your breath. I want to make the following couple of suggestions, neither of which will fundamentally change your situation. Your fundamental situation is that you are waiting, that you are holding your breath, and that you are scared to death. I completely understand. But I do have a couple of suggestions to make. Shall we look at them?

If your parent-client is in the middle of a crisis with her child, then her child is always on her mind. That is her reality. I'm presenting an extreme example by using World War II, but millions of parents are living with the felt crisis of a defiant child, a morose child, an unmotivated child, a sensitive child, a child doing poorly in school, and so on. Your client is struggling because her child is struggling. To help her, these twin struggles must be addressed.

The number of children being diagnosed with a mental disorder and being put on so-called psychiatric medication is increasing rapidly. What has happened? Primarily, certain ideas about "mental health" and "mental illness" have taken hold, promoted by special interest groups including psychiatrists, other mental health service providers, and pharmaceutical companies. That way of thinking became the dominant paradigm and continues as the dominant paradigm today. If you are a child and behave in certain ways that might plausibly have completely non-medical causes, you are nowadays routinely and immediately presumed to have a pseudo-medical-sounding affliction called a "mental disorder."

Beginning in the 1950s, mental health professionals announced that if you displayed certain behaviors or had certain thoughts or feelings called "symptoms" you had a "mental illness." Despite the fact that they made this claim without any scientific justification whatsoever, this claim stuck. It continues to stick today—still without any scientific justification. The "symptom picture" model took hold—and now it looks to have grabbed us by the throat. Although this model makes no scientific or logical sense, it is our current standard of care and an extraordinarily profitable cash cow for pharmaceutical companies, researchers, mental health professionals, and other vested interests.

Because this is the dominant paradigm and because it is touted everywhere, including in the media and by parents themselves, wherever parents turn they hear about little Bobby on attention deficit hyperactivity disorder (ADHD) medication or little Sally on a cocktail of meds for her childhood depression. Bombarded with news about this supposed mental disorder epidemic and about the rising rates of diagnosis and chemical use, if their own child shows certain unwanted behaviors, thoughts, or feelings they are bound suddenly to fear that they have a "mental patient in the making." What could feel more terrible? Naturally, feelings of helplessness, hopelessness, and failure well up as a parent's very connection to her child shifts from loving parent to frightened watchdog and prospective caretaker.

Employing Healthy Skepticism

Parents are bombarded on all sides—from mainstream media, school teachers and administrators, mental health professionals, pharmaceutical companies, and their own peers—with the following message. Something called "the mental disorders of childhood" exist and your child may well have one (or more) of them. Isn't your child restless? Isn't he squirming? Isn't he sad? Doesn't he say "no" a lot? All of these are symptoms of mental disorders! Watch out—your child probably has one!

Critics of the current paradigm have pointed out that the constructions of psychiatry are classic examples of pseudo-science employed to gain prestige, make money, and avoid the hard task of understanding what is actually going on in the mind and environment of a given child. Sharna Olfman, professor of clinical and developmental psychology at Point Park University, a psychologist in private practice, and the editor/author of the "Childhood in America" book series for Praeger Publishers, explained to me:

> Parents have been led to believe that popular childhood diagnoses such as ADHD and Bipolar Disorder are well understood illnesses that can be effectively treated with drugs that correct underlying chemical imbalances in the brain. In fact, even the former director of the National Institute of Mental Health, Dr. Thomas Insel, has stated publicly that DSM diagnoses [that is, diagnoses based on the American Psychiatric Association's Diagnostic and Statistical Manual of Mental Disorders] are premised on questionable science. Furthermore, not a single DSM diagnosis has been credibly linked to a chemical imbalance. While these widely held and highly persuasive beliefs are mere pseudoscience, there is a rich body of genetic and brain research with far reaching implications for diagnosis and treatment that has gone under the radar.

Dr. Brent Robbins is Chair of the Department of Humanities & Human Sciences at Point Park University and a past President of the Society for Humanistic Psychology, Division 32 of the American Psychological Association. Brent explained to me:

> The DSM-5 is the diagnostic manual that is produced by the American Psychiatric Association and is used by clinicians to diagnose people with various categories of mental illness. There is a growing concern that the diagnostic categories in the DSM-5 are not based on good science. The categories seem to lack reliability and validity. They lack reliability in that the same individual is likely to get diagnosed differently and inconsistently if he or she were to visit different clinicians. A good diagnostic instrument would, by contrast, lead to precision in diagnosis. The DSM-5 diagnostic categories, in most cases, are far below minimal expectations for reliability.

> The issue of validity is the concern that the DSM-5 diagnostic categories are often treated as if they point to underlying mental illnesses. But, in fact, we do not see evidence for this. Rather, DSM-5 diagnoses are descriptions of symptoms that often happen together, but they are not themselves an explanation for the symptoms that are being described. There are many reasons to be concerned about this beyond scientific concerns. The weakness of the DSM-5 has real implications for real lives. Because the instrument lacks scientific reliability and validity, many people get diagnosed and get put on medications when they don't merit a diagnosis and do not need the treatment. This puts the individual at risk of side effects from unnecessary treatment, and it takes resources away from individuals who really do need the treatment.
>
> It's important that both helpers and parents cast a skeptical eye at the psychiatric method and frankly doubt whether the current system of "diagnosing and treating the mental disorders of childhood" is a scientifically sound, helpful, or legitimate approach to dealing with children's feelings and behaviors.

What might a parent who is worried about his or her child do instead of or in addition to adopting the language and methods of the current mental disorder paradigm? There are a great many things that he or she might try and we will look at them as we proceed. To give you a first sense of these alternatives, here's Craig Wiener on the subject. Craig Wiener is a psychologist who wrote the book *Parenting Your Child with ADHD: A No-Nonsense Guide for Nurturing Self-Reliance and Cooperation*. Craig explained to me:

> There might be a variety of ways to account for why a child might qualify for the criteria of a mental health disorder. Instead of understanding their child's difficulties as a "chemical imbalance," which is what most traditional interventions presume, the parent might understand their child's behavior as their child's way of coping. Parents might observe and identify possible ways that day-to-day functioning reinforces the child's problematic behavior. Parents might then alter the sequence of events that are unwittingly perpetuating the unwanted patterns of behavior.

Likewise, parents might use less coercion and less reliance on external cues or directives when helping the child meet socio-cultural expectations; this helps to develop autonomy and independence. Parents might also incorporate their child's viewpoint as regularly as possible; this approach fosters amicable ways to resolve problems related to their child's integration with others. Parents might also set firmer limits on the extent to which they will accommodate their child's behaviors during times of troublesome responding, and thus require the child to meet them halfway. And parents can role model the behaviors they want their child to imitate.

It will make a huge positive difference in your client's life—and in her child's life—if you let her know about these sorts of parenting alternatives, if you help her acquire more effective parenting skills, and if you articulate what upgrading her family's dynamics might look like. If she were to make these changes, they of course might or might not prove sufficient. You are offering your client no silver bullets or guarantees. But, by the same token, they just might prove tremendously beneficial—and help prevent both parent and child from having to go down the road of a lifelong diagnostic label and powerful, problematic chemicals. Wouldn't that prove a blessing?

Addressing Parents Directly

It hurts a parent's heart to see his or her child in distress. Hardly anything hurts more. That hurt is compounded by the powerlessness that parents feel. We are powerless to "cure" our children. Powerlessness is a sure road to sadness and feeling overwhelmed. You want your child to be happy and healthy; your child is anything but; yet you can't snap your fingers and make him or her better.

If what ailed your child were anything like a broken ankle, you would know exactly what to do and where to go. You would go to a medical doctor and get your child's ankle cast. But what does one "do" with an odd child, an angry child, an anxious child, a moody child, an obsessive child, a withdrawn child, an addicted child, or an out-of-control child? For that child, what is the equivalent of casting their broken ankle? And who should do the casting? Who is the right "doctor" for this sort of problem?

Let's say that you are the parent of an angry child who is in emotional pain, who is acting out and making it incredibly difficult for you to feel loving toward him or her, and who rejects your helping advances. At the same time, you can't help but feel that you or your circumstances must have contributed to all this anger and pain—on top of feeling helpless, you also feel guilty. Then, in addition to the difficulties your child is experiencing and the guilt you are carrying, comes the third strike. You look for some help and you are advised (or commanded) to enter our mental health system.

Our mental health system, with its particular way of making up a label for what your son or daughter is experiencing and its penchant for offering up chemicals as your child's best hope, steps in, labels your child, and starts its regimen of chemicals. Maybe you are relieved that your child has been "diagnosed" and is now receiving "medical help." Maybe you are rather doubtful about this "diagnosis" and suspicious of a "chemical cure." In either case, you may soon find that your situation is worse rather than better. Now you may find yourself living two nightmares instead of one: the nightmare of your child's difficulties and the nightmare of insufficient and perhaps downright dangerous "solutions."

Let's try to tease apart the many difficulties that make this picture so poignant, painful, and maddening for parents.

First—and as you quite possibly realize very clearly in your gut—no one really knows what is going on. Your child does not know. You do not know. No mental health professional really knows (though they may claim to know). What if your son is harboring some deep-seated sorrow or has turned his anxious feelings and his natural childhood awkwardness into a hatred of life? How could this be known with any certainty? What if your daughter has been battling with her sister all of her life without anyone being quite aware of the damage done to her by this daily warfare? How could this be known with any certainty? What if a seemingly small thing has happened that has produced out-sized consequences? How could this be known with any certainty?

Second, we do not know what part a child's natural endowments are playing. We do not know the contours of any child's original personality or how that original personality is making itself felt in that child's forming (and formed) personality. We do not know how the mind he arrived with actually works. Surely that really must matter—and we do not know anything about that. What difficulties will him possessing a high intelligence likely or inevitably produce? What difficulties will him coming into the world already addicted likely or inevitably produce? What difficulties will him being born a "feminine" boy or being born a "masculine" girl likely or inevitably produce? Mustn't "who we are" matter?

Third, we do not know what part "biology" plays in all this. When "biology" is introduced into a discussion of this sort as a possible explanation, typically the following is meant. Maybe this crisis isn't "psychological" or "social" or "environmental" or "familial" but is instead the result of something being broken or out of whack. For example, maybe there is a "chemical imbalance" or a "genetic" explanation for the crisis. "Biology" used this way naturally leads to ideas like "mental illness" and "mental disorder." That "biology" in this sense is implicated is not at all known. To many it seems logical that it must be implicated and to others it seems completely illogical. But who knows?

Fourth, we simply can't get into another person's head. A child is somebody with an inner life. Children think, imagine, feel, dream, remember, and hope. But we can't get "inside there" to see all that thinking, imagining, feeling, dreaming, remembering, and hoping or to see how our child is constructing his or her reality. How do trips to church to hear a pastor decry homosexuality combine with a child's budding guilty feelings of attraction to members of the same sex? How does being told by one parent that you are special and being told by the other parent that you are worthless "come together" in a child's psyche? If only we could know what was going on in there! But we can't.

Fifth—and this is very difficult to talk about—what if you are a significant part of the problem? What if your mate is? What if another one of your children is? What if the visceral anger between you and your mate is making your child anxious? What if, just to make ends meet, you must stay so busy and so unavailable that your child feels abandoned? That is, to what extent will your desire to help your child be compromised by your defensiveness around the part you may be playing in her difficulties? This defensiveness is such a human problem and such a human reality! Can you reduce your defensiveness and change your part in the equation?

Sixth, your child may not have the problem—your culture and society may have the problem. If, for example, many or most of the typical features of childhood, from squirming to feeling anxious to defying authority, are deemed "symptoms of a mental disorder"—and that is the current trend—then your unfortunate child will become "abnormal" and "different" by definition. Once defined that way, he (and you) will have to deal with a system that has a particular way of "treating" what it has defined as "disordered," a way dominated by chemicals with powerful effects called "medication." This is just one of the many ways that culture and society may be making problems for your child and your family.

Seventh, we don't know what, if anything, can counteract the damage done by early trauma. If, for example, a given infant feels abandoned, experiences what is called "insecure attachment," and learns not to trust, not to care, and not to love, what will help the most or help at all to rewire that child into a trusting, caring, loving human being? We hate the idea of having to reply, "Nothing"; nor do we know if "nothing" is the right answer. Maybe multiple efforts, including loving parenting, supportive psychotherapy, compassionate mentoring, focused life skills training, and some real-world successes might heal and transform him. But we do not know.

Eighth—and this flows from the preceding seven points—we aren't very clear on what helps or what helps in a given situation. Maybe "talking it out" with a trained listener like a psychotherapist can help—but to what extent can that really help if what is going on is connected to some aspect of your child's original personality or to some stressor that is out of your child's control to change, like a tumultuous or traumatic family situation? When is something like "talk" appropriate or even relevant, even if the

> talk is "expert"? Given how little clarity we have about what actually helps, it's important that we look at a given child's distress through multiple lenses and with many different sorts of help in mind. We will do exactly that shortly.

Currently parents are bombarded by the mainstream view, promoted by pharmaceutical companies, academic researchers, mental health professionals, professional organizations, a naïve or indifferent media, and their own friends and family members, that "mental disorders" exist in the same way that "physical disorders" exist. Likewise, they are told that if their child is afflicted with one of these "mental disorders," the only real help available are chemicals and, in a secondary way, a certain kind of "expert talk" called psychotherapy. However, these are not the only ways to look at the matter.

Advocates of a critical psychology approach suggest that there are other ways to conceptualize what's going on and other helpful approaches to take. As a wise and humane helper, you can present these alternative views to your clients. That isn't to say, however, that your client is certain to be pleased with your brand of helping. Some parents may be very happy that, for example, their "disruptive" child has received a mental disorder diagnosis—that they now "know what's going on"—and they may likewise be very happy that "doctors are doing something for our child."

They may swear by the chemicals that their child is being given, grateful for the short-term ameliorating effects, and not overly concerned about any lasting side effects or about opening pathways to addiction. Your client may be one of these and may strongly oppose any other point of view and reject the information you're providing. So, not only am I asking a lot of you, that you actively paint a picture of alternatives to the current paradigm—your client may be anything but grateful when you do so.

Nevertheless, I think that it is our job and our duty to invite the parents we work with to think about their child's distress from a "critical" point of view. Does this amount to a certain sort of activism? Yes, it does. Is this you being rather directive? Yes, it is. Is this you functioning in part as a teacher? Yes, indeed. Might you have to tell clients some hard truths about their part in the problem? Yes, you might. Does this require that you craft talking points about the current diagnostic system and the use of psychiatric medication? Yes, it does. But if you would like to help your clients who are also parents, I hope that you'll agree that all of this is required of you. Parents are under siege—and you are in a position to help them. Indeed, there is hardly anyone in a better position.

> **Pressured Parents**
>
> If the instruments of society—your child's pediatrician, your child's teacher, your child's principal, your child's guidance counselor, etc.—suggest, imply, or announce that your child has a mental disorder, that he or she ought to be treated as soon as possible with a regimen of chemicals, and that to do otherwise is irresponsible on your part, endangers your child's future in school and in life, and is tantamount to child neglect, how can you be expected to think clearly about what's going on, research alternatives, or not succumb to that enormous pressure?
>
> When the deck is stacked against you and your child in such powerful ways, how can you successfully resist or calmly proceed?
>
> Step one is to recognize that you *are* being pressured. If someone in a position of power or a supposed expert provides you with exactly one explanation of what is going on—the mental disorder explanation—and you *know* that there are and must be multiple ways to conceptualize what's going on, you should appreciate that their "one explanation" amounts to implicit pressure to believe a certain thing, to react in a certain way, and to grant the powers that be a certain blanket permission. You are having the experience of being pressured because you *are* being pressured. Internally nod and say, "What I'm feeling is real. They are pressuring me!"

Every mental health helper or wellness helper—every psychotherapist, psychiatrist, mental health counselor, wellness coach, nurse, general practitioner, family therapist—numbers parents among her clients or patients.

Even if, as a helper, you are not directly working with children, you are working with their parents all the time. And if your client who happens to be a parent is dealing with a distressed or diagnosed child—and millions of parents are—that reality may be the most pressing challenge and the most significant stressor in your client's life.

Therefore, you need a good working knowledge of what parents and children are currently experiencing and practiced ways of interacting with those suffering parents. Likewise, if you have your doubts that the current mental disorder paradigm really serves parents and their children, you will want to know how to deliver help from a critical psychological perspective.

When a client comes in for help with any sort of issue—despair, anxiety, addiction, work issues, relationship issues—if he or she is also the parent of a distressed or diagnosed child, that amounts to a significant challenge that helpers are obliged to address. Whether her child is four years old, 14 years old, or 40 years old, his presence in her life is a profound, poignant, and pressing part of her current reality.

1

DIAGNOSING OR LABELING?

Parents need help to understand what "diagnosing" means (and doesn't mean) when it comes to so-called mental disorders and to the current mental disorder paradigm as undergirded by the Diagnostic & Statistical Manual of the American Psychiatric Association (DSM) and the International Classification of Diseases (ICD). They are likely to think that something like medicine is going on because words like "disorder" and "treatment" and "medication" are being used. They are unlikely to be able to see that nothing like medicine is actually going on.

What is going on? Let's take a look. Imagine that you got upset. Is it very remarkable that I can "diagnose" that you are upset? After all, you are clearly upset. What expert thing did I accomplish by agreeing with you that you were upset? Or imagine that you are angry. Is it very remarkable that I can "diagnose" that you are angry? After all, you are clearly angry. Have I added anything meaningful by saying "I diagnose that you are angry" instead of "You seem angry"?

"You look upset" is the simple, truthful thing to say and "I diagnose that you look upset" is a piece of self-serving chicanery. By adopting that circumlocution I've tried to turn an ordinary observation into a pseudo-scientific marvel. If this is the way I'm operating, I dearly hope that you won't notice my little game.

By contrast, let's say that you explain to me that you've been having hallucinations. You describe the look of your hallucination and you also describe to me your recent history, other physical symptoms, and so on. Taking that information together, I have a strong hunch that you're suffering from early Parkinson's. I then run tests to confirm or disconfirm my hypothesis. I didn't "diagnose" your hallucination—you handed me that. I diagnosed your Parkinson's.

We seem to have a lot of trouble understanding this difference: the difference between "diagnosing a symptom" and "diagnosing a cause." The second is what medicine legitimately does. The first is what the mental health establishment illegitimately does. It is not real diagnosis for me to "diagnose you with an anxiety disorder" because you told me you were anxious. This is chicanery and not diagnosis.

You don't diagnose symptoms. You diagnose causes. To diagnose a symptom is only to say, "Yes, I agree, you have a rash." Everyone who looks at you knows that you have a rash! What we want to know is what sort of rash it is. What's causing it? You observe the tumor and you diagnose the cancer. You observe the bump and you diagnose the concussion. You observe the fever and you diagnose the influenza. You don't observe the anxiety and diagnose the anxiety. That is wrong.

You observe a symptom, you interpret a symptom, and you make use of a symptom as part of your efforts at diagnosis. But the symptom isn't the diagnosis. You observe a symptom and then you diagnose a cause. *You don't observe anxiety and then diagnose anxiety.* It isn't okay to call this "diagnosing." It isn't okay to turn a report of anxiety into "an anxiety disorder" just by saying so. Yet this is what is done all the time nowadays.

Here, for example, are some of the questions whose positive answer will get you an "anxiety disorder" diagnosis:

- "Are you feeling keyed up or on edge?": that is, are you feeling anxious?

- "Do you have feelings of panic, fear, or uneasiness?": that is, are you feeling anxious?
- "Are you constantly worrying about small or large concerns?": that is, are you feeling anxious?
- "Are you constantly tense": that is, are you feeling anxious?
- "Does your anxiety interfere with your work, school, or family responsibilities?": that is, are you feeling anxious?
- "Are you plagued by fears that you know are irrational, but can't shake?": that is, are you feeling anxious?
- "Do you avoid everyday situations or activities because they cause you anxiety?": that is, are you feeling anxious?
- "Do you watch for signs of danger?": that is, are you feeling anxious?

If you answer yes to these questions, you are acknowledging in these different-but-same ways that you are feeling anxious. But what you get from the mental health establishment is not, "Yes, you are clearly feeling anxious. Let's see if we can figure out why." What you get is a "diagnosis" of an "anxiety disorder." In our current system, you appear to have "eight symptoms" of an "anxiety disorder." You come in looking anxious, acting anxious, and saying that you are anxious. What sort of "diagnostic acumen" does it take for me to say, "You're anxious"?

Parents need help in understanding this. This is what is going on when a mental health professional tells a parent that little Johnny has "seven symptoms of ADHD" and therefore "has ADHD" and therefore ought to be "put on medication for his ADHD." This sounds like medicine but it is not.

Interview with Sami Timimi

Sami Timimi is a consultant Child and Adolescent Psychiatrist who is Director of Medical Education at Lincolnshire Partnership Foundation, NHS Trust, and Visiting Professor of Child Psychiatry and Mental Health Improvement on the faculty of Health and Social Sciences at Lincoln University. He is the author of *Naughty Boys: Anti-Social Behaviour, ADHD and the Role of Culture*, *A Straight-Talking*

Introduction to *Children's Mental Health* and *The Myth of Autism: Medicalising Men's and Boys' Social and Emotional Competence.*

Eric Maisel: How would you suggest a parent thinks about being told that his or her child meets the criteria for a mental disorder or a mental illness diagnosis?

Sami Timimi: It is essential to understand that in psychiatry there is no such thing as "diagnosis." Diagnosis in medicine refers to the process of understanding how a person's symptoms relate to an underlying disease process. Diagnosis is a technical process in which a medical practitioner identifies a possible cause or causes of a patient's complaints. Making the correct diagnosis in medicine is essential for choosing the correct treatment.

In psychiatry, we have a number of systems for classification of people's complaints, but we do not have diagnoses. The classifications we use are descriptive (they describe the patient's problems) but not diagnostic (they tell us nothing about the possible causes of those problems) and therefore do not aid decision-making for treatment and may lead to worse outcomes if the classifications are used as if they are diagnostic.

Consider the following comparison. If, for example, I was to ask the question "What is attention deficit hyperactivity disorder (ADHD)?" then in our current state of knowledge it isn't possible for me to answer that question by reference to any particular known biological abnormality. Instead I will have to provide a description; in other words ADHD is the presence of hyperactivity, impulsivity, and poor attention (plus a few extra qualifiers such as age of onset).

Contrast this with asking the question "What is diabetes?" If I were to answer this question in the same manner that I answered the question about ADHD, by just describing symptoms such as needing to urinate frequently, thirst, and fatigue, I could be in deep trouble as a medical practitioner as there are plenty of other conditions that may initially present with a similar picture and indeed diabetes itself may not present with these symptoms in a recognizable way.

To answer the question "What is diabetes?" I have to refer to the biological cause of abnormalities in sugar metabolism. My task is then to carry out biological tests (such as analyzing the blood and/or urine for levels of glucose) that provide me with empirical data that is independent of my subjective opinion to help support (or not) my hypothesis about possible causes of the patient's behavior. In this situation, my diagnosis explains the behaviors/symptoms that are described, and is vital for choosing the correct treatment.

In psychiatry, what is referred to as "diagnosis" will only describe but cannot explain. This can be further illustrated by considering what happens if we try to use a psychiatric diagnosis to explain. If, for example, I were to ask why a particular child can't concentrate, is hyperactive, and shows impulsivity and I were to answer that it is because they have ADHD, then a legitimate question to ask is "How do you know it is because they have ADHD?" The only answer I can give is that I know it's ADHD because the child is presenting with hyperactivity, impulsivity, and poor attention. Thus, we end up with a circular argument where the behaviors are caused by the behaviors. It's a bit like saying my headache is caused by a pain in the head.

Not only is it essential to understand that there is no such thing as diagnosis in psychiatry, but it's also important to understand the problem of "reliability" in psychiatric classification. "Reliability" refers to the likelihood that different doctors seeing the same person with the same description of their problems will reach the same conclusion about their diagnosis/classification.

Reliability when it comes to psychiatric "diagnoses" is very poor. This means that whatever classification you get often has more to do with who you see, what country you are in, who has trained them, and so on, than what the actual problems being reported are. As a result, there are wide variations within countries and between countries in the numbers being "diagnosed" with labels like ADHD, autism, and depression. Furthermore, a "diagnosis" once given in psychiatry is often not taken away, but rather, if problems persist, new ones are added, thus it is not uncommon for those who attend mental health services long term to "collect" several "diagnoses."

In brief, then, in psychiatry we have a system for classification and not diagnoses. The classifications can be helpful (for example to validate suffering or to access resources) but they cannot be used to explain behaviors and experiences and therefore

> cannot help with finding the approach or treatment that will prove most helpful. As psychiatric classifications have poor reliability, the diagnoses you receive has more to do with the doctor you see than the problem you have and if your problems continue you become vulnerable to receiving more "diagnoses" with all the consequences this may bring.
>
> As a parent, you should normalize your view of suffering. Western culture, perhaps as a result of advances in healthcare, pain management, temperature regulation of our buildings, and so on, has much greater intolerance toward mental suffering than many other cultures. We now view growing up as a process loaded with risk and are more likely than ever to feel that it needs experts, like myself, to "know" what kids need to grow up mentally healthy.
>
> In the past few decades our trust in who had the best knowledge on how to help kids grow up changed from being our own parents, grandparents, and communities to professionals. As a result, the trials and tribulations of growing up have been increasingly "medicalized" and turned into "disorders" that are sometimes "treated" with medications that have been given names like "anti-depressant" to give the marketing illusion that they have specific properties that treat a disease.
>
> Growing up is not a pain-free process and I encourage everyone involved in looking after kids to focus less on their vulnerabilities and more on celebrating and recognizing their strengths, talents, and skills (whatever these may be) and resisting the idea that there is something mentally "defective" or "disordered" about their child that sets them apart from the rest of us.

For the many professionals who are looking for decent alternatives to the current mental health labeling system and to our methods of diagnosing, I would say that the best alternative is not to diagnose at all. Let us understand diagnosing for what it is: an inappropriate lifting of a term and an idea from enterprises where it makes sense, like repairing cars and repairing hearts, to one where it doesn't. We will do much better as helpers without adding illegitimate "diagnosing" to our game plan.

A lawyer helps his client without also diagnosing him or labeling him. An accountant helps his client without diagnosing him or labeling him. A mental health professional can help his clients without also diagnosing or labeling them. If they are suffering from a medical illness, they should see a doctor, who has the job of diagnosing their diabetes or Parkinson's. Diagnosing those real illnesses isn't the job of any psychotherapist on earth. Nor should it be their job to "diagnose" made-up "mental disorders."

By the Way: What *Is* a Mental Disorder?

No one doubts that phenomena like sadness and worry exist. But to call them symptoms of mental disorders is a fraudulent leap. We shouldn't illegitimately use real phenomena as "proof" of the existence of non-existing things.

It is certainly easy for the definers of non-existing mental disorders to define a mental disorder any way they like, since they are not defining any real thing. For example, they defined a mental disorder in the following way in the DSM-IV:

> A mental disorder is a clinically significant behavioral or psychological syndrome or pattern that occurs in an individual and that is associated with present distress or disability or with a significantly increased risk of suffering death, pain, disability, or an important loss of freedom.

Then, under pressure from skeptics as to whether this definition made any sense whatsoever, they redefined these non-existing mental disorders this new way in the DSM-5:

> A mental disorder is a syndrome characterized by clinically significant disturbance in an individual's cognitions, emotion regulation, or behavior that reflects a dysfunction in the psychological, biological, or developmental processes underlying mental functioning. Mental disorders are usually associated with significant distress in social, occupational, or other important activities. An expectable or culturally approved

> response to a common stressor or loss, such as the death of a loved one, is not a mental disorder. Socially deviant behavior (e.g., political or sexual) and conflicts that are primarily between the individual and society are not mental disorders unless the deviance or conflict results from a dysfunction in the individual, as described above.

The very idea that you can radically change the definition of something without anything in the real world changing and with no new increases in knowledge or understanding is remarkable—remarkable only until you realize that the thing being defined does not exist. It is completely easy—effortless, really—to change the definition of something that does not exist to suit your current purposes. In fact, there is hardly any better proof of the non-existence of a non-existing thing than that you can define it one way today, another way tomorrow, and a third way on Sunday.

One could scrutinize these changes and make reasonable comments about the way that language has been employed to say absolutely nothing. A mental disorder is a psychological thing, or maybe it isn't. A mental disorder is a biological thing, or maybe it isn't. You can rail about your society unless you have a "dysfunction," at which point your railing is a mental disorder. You can have a conflict with your politicians unless you have a "dysfunction," at which point you are a mental deviant. One could go on with such observations, but making them plays into the hands of the creators of non-existing things, who love it when you play their game. They can slip about with impunity, adding, qualifying, and shifting, while you waste your breath being reasonable and thoughtful.

The question is not, "What is the best definition of a mental disorder?" The question is not, "Is the DSM-5 definition of a mental disorder better than the DSM-IV definition of a mental disorder?" Those are absolutely not the right questions. The first and only question is, "Do mental disorders actually exist?" The phenomena certainly exist: pain and suffering certainly exist. But turning them into so-called mental disorders via linguistic tricks shouldn't fly.

The end of diagnosing, if that feat could be pulled off, certainly wouldn't imply the end of helping. It would imply the end of "treating," another medical word and medical idea; but it would actually promote rather than impede helping. In a post-diagnosis future, you could say,

> You're anxious. Let's investigate why, because maybe that investigation will help us. And if we can't figure out why, that's okay too. We can still try out some things that may help you feel less anxious. And, who knows, they may even help with what's causing the anxiety. Okay? By the way, I will need your cooperation in this because I am not a doctor with tests and treatments and what have you. I am just a person like you. I'm willing to focus you a little, ask some pointed questions, be on your side when I feel I can be, and be "in this" with you. But I need your help. Okay?

That is, can we be of help even if we can't locate the "cause" of sadness or anxiety? Of course we can. You can "treat a symptom" without "diagnosing that symptom." This happens all the time in medicine. You call your doctor late in the afternoon and say, "I have a headache." He says, "Take two aspirins and call me in the morning." He has not diagnosed you but he is treating your symptom; and history tells him that you will probably wake up without the headache for any one of three reasons: that the aspirin worked, that some placebo effect worked, or that the headache, like many headaches, just went away.

It is perfectly plausible, sensible, and reasonable to sometimes "just treat symptoms"—but that doesn't mean that we aren't interested in causes!

We have plenty of things to recommend that might help a sad person, an anxious person, a person drinking alcoholically, and so on. Maybe a sad person would benefit from some sunlight, an anxious person from some "don't sweat the small stuff" training, a problem drinker from AA. But if the headaches persist, you don't just keep "treating the symptom"—you don't just keep recommending aspirins. You say to the person across from you, "Please, please, please, let's see if we can get at what's going on here. Okay? Can we please do a little investigating?"

A helper can do both: you can "treat the symptom" by providing some time-tested tactics and you can also "investigate what's going on underneath." Indeed, this amounts to best practice. And nowhere in this best practice was there a need for diagnosing to rear its ugly head.

Yet many well-meaning mental health professionals retain a desire to diagnose because they genuinely believe in the "diagnosing and treating" model. A well-known therapist dropped me the following note in response to a column of mine in Psychology Today:

> I appreciate your position and understand your concern about using the word "diagnosis," but I think it is unfortunate that we have ceded this term entirely to medical practice. According to Merriam Webster's dictionary, diagnosis is the "investigation or analysis of the cause or nature of a condition, situation, or problem." By this definition, mental health disorder categories may not even qualify as diagnoses because by being "atheoretical" regarding cause, they offer little in terms of meaningful explanation that lends itself to helpful courses of action.
>
> Psychological formulation, on the other hand, fits nicely with the idea of diagnosis as a process by which we come to identify and understand the problems clients present to their therapists. I'd go so far as to say that based on this definition, client and counselor could even diagnose a problem together—something quite different from the usual presumption that diagnosis is limited to the notion of expert therapists independently deciding what is wrong without client involvement. My point is that diagnosis need not be viewed in the very restricted sense it has been for so long in the helping professions.

I understand this desire, but this would still amount to a misuse of the word "diagnosis" and it would continue our current pattern of abusing both language and human beings. You discern causes, if you can; you don't co-create them. A helper and her client can certainly co-create a plan for managing anxiety, co-create an agreement about what the client will or won't try, and so on. All of that can be co-created. But you can't co-create a diagnosis. That's Monty Python territory.

Interview with Gary Greenberg

Gary Greenberg practices psychotherapy in Connecticut. He is a contributing editor for Harper's Magazine and the author of four books, including Manufacturing Depression: The Secret History of a Modern Disease and The Book of Woe: The DSM and the Unmaking of Psychiatry.

Eric Maisel: Most parents will only have a glancing understanding of what the DSM is (if even that) or why it's so important as part of the current, dominant mental health paradigm of "diagnosing and treating mental disorders." What is the DSM?

Gary Greenberg: The DSM, the Diagnostic and Statistical Manual of Mental Disorders, is the American Psychiatric Association's compendium of psychiatric diagnoses. It lays out, dictionary-like, all the mental illnesses recognized by the American Psychiatric Association (APA), and the criteria by which they are known. Designed to provide a universal language for psychiatry, it is used by clinicians and researchers around the world. As a result of its predominance, the DSM's categories and concepts frame the discussion, within the mental health professions and in the general public, of mental suffering. When a person in casual conversation describes herself as "totally OCD," or when a teacher suggests to parents that they have their child evaluated for ADHD, they are, generally without knowing it, drawing on the DSM's categories.

EM: What do you see as the flaws regarding the DSM?

GG: The DSM is very good at what it explicitly sets out to be good at, which is systematically describing the ways people suffer. A clinician tells another clinician that a patient has paranoid schizophrenia; assuming the diagnosis is made carefully, and assuming the second clinician is familiar with the diagnosis, then it is likely that useful information has been transmitted. Similarly, if a researcher publishes a paper about bipolar disorder, then it is safe to assume that he or she is writing about the same collection of symptoms that are the subject of other papers on bipolar disorder.

The DSM, in other words, has scientific reliability (although not as much as is generally thought, and less in the DSM-5 than in recent editions). But it does not have scientific validity. The categories in it are constructs; there is no evidence that, for example, major depressive disorder exists in the same way that, say, diabetes or cancer exist. The disorders are purely heuristic. This aspect of the DSM, which is acknowledged by the APA, becomes a flaw when the diagnoses are reified and people—clinicians and the public alike—begin to think of them as real. At that point, what is, at best, an anthropology of mental suffering becomes a pseudo-science.

This outcome is not accidental, or the result of ignorance. Since the third edition came out in 1980, its implicit purpose has been to provide scientific respectability to psychiatry, which has long suffered from "physics envy." The DSM-III adopted a scientific rhetoric, but without providing an actual scientific basis for its rendering of the world of mental illness. This move succeeded in restoring the credibility of psychiatry, but the authority it derives as a result is not really backed up by the kind of science that backs up, say, cancer research. Psychiatry's reach, as embodied in the DSM, exceeds its grasp.

EM: *You write about "manufacturing depression." What do you mean by that phrase and what are you implying by that phrase?*

GG: The idea that depression is an illness—the major depressive disorder of the DSM—is a good example of what is wrong with the DSM. To call the heterogeneous experience of depression a disease is to make a set of claims about the nature and causes of unhappiness that has profound implications. The diagnosis is the gateway not only to taking antidepressants or other treatments for a "disease"; it is also the gateway to a certain kind of understanding of oneself and one's suffering. If you are told by a person with authority that you have a biochemical imbalance that is causing your depression, you are also being told, among other things, that your suffering is not the result of anything in the external world, that it is incumbent on you to heal yourself, and that your mind is no more or less than what your brain does.

This very consequential idea is not the result of a scientific discovery. Rather, it is a historical development, the convergence of a number of political, social, and economic forces. To say it is manufactured is not to say that it is a conspiracy, but instead to give people a way of understanding this very powerful idea, to put it in context so that when and if you get depressed, you can decide to what extent you want to buy it.

EM: *If you could snap your fingers and change the current mental health system and/or overthrow the current mental disorder paradigm, what would you change and/or overthrow?*

> GG: I think therapists should stop pretending that we are treating illnesses, starting with decoupling ourselves from the DSM. The vast majority of therapists use the DSM in the most cynical way—as a means to getting paid. Ask yourself: if there wasn't an insurance company involved would you make a diagnosis? And once you've made the diagnosis, of what value is it in the actual treatment?
>
> Using the DSM means that many if not most therapeutic encounters start with a lie—that the client has a mental illness. Not that I think we're obligated to be truthful with insurance companies, but this is more than a little ironic: an encounter that is supposed to be about honesty has dishonesty at its foundation. More to the point, however, starting off with a diagnosis, even one that is disavowed, cannot help but affect the therapeutic relationship, even if in very subtle ways.
>
> So, I think we should at the very least level with our clients from the beginning. Tell them you are diagnosing them with a mental illness. Explain why, and which one, and remind them that this diagnosis will follow them throughout their lives. Give them the option of not getting diagnosed. Of course, this means that they will have to pay out-of-pocket, which in turn means that you will probably get paid substantially less money. So, you will both have to decide what therapy is worth to you.
>
> Pulling on this thread may begin to unravel the tapestry of psychotherapy as we practice it now. That might not be a bad thing. It might take us out from under the medical paradigm, where we don't exactly belong. But in return, it might place us on a more solid foundation to do what many of us got into the business to do—to help people find the meaning and value in their lives, which is a different endeavor from helping them cure their mental illnesses.

The challenge for any contemporary psychotherapist who wants to retain an ability to "diagnose and treat" is simple to describe: give me an example of your updated diagnostic system. Tell me how you would test to confirm your diagnoses and how you would distinguish one cause or source of a problem from another cause or source of a problem. Give me your taxonomy—your naming system and your rationale for using it—and let's hold it up to scrutiny. If you want to continue diagnosing, put up the names of your "mental disorders" and let's look them over. And don't forget to indicate clearly what you are counting as causes! If you don't take causes into account, you still aren't really diagnosing. You are merely cataloguing.

I think that we will discover, if we are truthful and if we are acting in good faith, that it is impossible to retain the idea of "diagnosing" when it comes to human experiences. We should stop "diagnosing symptoms" right now, as that is a completely illegitimate enterprise that is annually adding millions of people, many of them children, to the rolls of the "mentally disordered." This should stop today. But we should also let go of the idea that "diagnosing and treating" makes any sense in the context of human experience. It is this simple: we have adopted the wrong model. It is past time to discard it.

As to whether there is perhaps some way to retain the idea of "diagnosing," let those who want it retained describe what their taxonomy might look like and let us see if we believe them. I don't think we will believe them, because it is folly, and always will be folly, to "diagnose the human condition" when we have no way of knowing what counts as cause-and-effect in human affairs. Are we to "diagnose" personality differences, changed circumstances, stray and odd thoughts, and every single human thing, from war breaking out to a month of cloudy days? Such an enterprise makes no sense.

We do not know what has caused a given adult or child to become anxious, and while we can investigate his situation with him we can't arrive at the sorts of conclusions that in medicine are called "diagnoses." To announce that we can arrive at such conclusions or that such conclusions are warranted by our investigations is to lie. We can help that adult or child a lot—and we will help him a lot more if we stop "diagnosing" him and simply start helping him. That should be our rallying cry: "Lots of help and no more diagnosing!"

A doctor is not engaged in idle investigating. He is trying to *succeed* in his investigations. We do not think that a doctor has been successful who engages in one surgery after another to find out "what is wrong with us." In that unfortunate set of circumstances, he has not reached a conclusion yet and so he can't make a diagnosis. If there ever was a way to "diagnose" in human affairs—and there never will be—we would need to set the bar exactly that high: we would need to be *successful* in our investigations and we would need to be able to say, "This is clearly causing that." That time can never come.

A diagnosis is a *conclusion* about cause and effect. "You need new spark plugs" is a conclusion about cause and effect. "You say you are anxious so I will say that you are anxious" is not a conclusion about cause and effect. It is time for society, in the form of its legislators and watchdogs, to end this travesty. Millions upon millions of adults and children are receiving "diagnoses" that make no earthly sense. And these "diagnoses" stay with them forever. Mention that you are sad to the wrong person and you will carry a "clinical depression" label with you everywhere.

It is time we placed a moratorium on this illegitimate "diagnosing." No new system will prove legitimate because we do not actually know what "causes" individual human experiences like sadness and anxiety. It is simply improper to turn human experiences, even of the most painful and the most unwanted sort, into "disorders." Let us help with the pain; let us really help the people who are suffering.

2

DECONSTRUCTING ATTENTION DEFICIT HYPERACTIVITY DISORDER

In this chapter, we'll look at one of the more common "mental disorders of childhood," so-called attention deficit hyperactivity disorder (ADHD).

I hope that you'll be able to let go of your indoctrination in the mental disorder paradigm, the DSM, and the pseudo-medical way of thinking about what's going on when a child can't sit still very well and open up to the following four realities: (1) That there is no scientific evidence that these behaviors amount to a so-called mental disorder; (2) that there is no logic to bundling symptoms and calling them mental disorders; (3) that we do not know what is going on until we investigate (and even after investigating we may not know); and (4) that there are other approaches to dealing with this "hyperactivity" than applying powerful chemicals.

One of the most common "mental disorders" to anoint a child with nowadays is "attention deficit hyperactivity disorder." This is the "diagnosis" you get if you squirm. This diagnosis comes in different flavors—you can be "predominantly impulsive," "predominantly inattentive," and so on—and these different flavors exist so as to make sure that every possible feature of childhood is captured by one label or another. The unstated goal is rather clear: to turn childhood itself into a mental disorder.

Of course, this "diagnosing" and subsequent "treatment" of children with powerful, addictive chemicals that resemble our "war on crime" street drugs are at once bizarre and, if the powerful could be held accountable, felonious. Yet parents seem hard pressed to say no to the idea that common, understandable features of childhood should be called mental disorders for no medical or logical reasons.

But He Was Tested

One reason that parents are led to believe that "mental disorders" like ADHD exist is that "you can test for them." But what is actually going on with regard to such so-called testing?

If it has been suggested (or even virtually mandated) that your child be "tested for ADHD," what does that mean? What exactly is being "tested"? It's vital to understand that a test is worthless—and very likely dangerous—if the underlying construct is invalid. For your child to have an "attention deficit hyperactivity disorder," there must be such a thing as an "attention deficit hyperactivity disorder."

It wouldn't matter if there were a hundred tests to support the notion that you had something if that something didn't really exist. Creating a test to support a given construct is child's play. That the test exists says nothing about the validity of the construct.

A test may indicate or "prove" that your child is sad. But that is not a test for the "mental disorder of depression" unless there is a "mental disorder of depression." A test may indicate or "prove" that your child is anxious. But that is not a test for the "mental disorder of generalized anxiety" unless there is a "mental disorder of generalized anxiety." A test may indicate or "prove" that your child is not interested in what he is not interested in and that he squirms when he is not interested. But that is not a test for the "mental disorder of attention deficit hyperactivity disorder" unless there is a "mental disorder" of "attention deficit hyperactivity disorder."

In our current system, you are put in the position of trusting that the establishment is doing an honorable job of identifying conditions that exist rather than pinning labels on sets of "symptoms" so as to create a cash flow. Is that honorable job being done? Many critics of the system do not believe that it is. It is a shame that you have the job of being a detective in addition to the hard-enough job of being a parent.

As a mind experiment, consider the following. I can easily make up a "mental disorder" and then create a test to test for it. Let's say that it serves me to call "eating your ice cream before your peas" a mental disorder. Let's call that a "sweet compulsion disorder." Next, I create a test to see if you prefer to eat your ice cream first or your peas first (and if you are a child, which are you likely to pick?). Creating that test would be a snap. I would simply ask you in 15 or 20 different ways whether you prefer ice cream to peas, say by changing the flavor of the ice cream in each question: "Do you prefer eating chocolate ice cream to peas?"; "Do you prefer eating strawberry ice cream to peas?"; and so on. That's all there is to it. With this test in hand, I can prove that you have a "sweet compulsion disorder." Just like that.

Since, if I am a mental health professional with bills to pay and ties to big pharma, I may be out to cast a wide net and get as many children as possible labeled with this disorder, I'll construct the test so that it is hard not to choose "ice cream first" (as if, if you're a child, you're likely to make some other choice!). At the end of this illegitimate process, I may brazenly say to you, the parent, "We have tested your child and he definitely has a sweet compulsion disorder." Will you see through this ruse? Can you really be expected to see through it? And aren't mental health professionals currently relying on you not questioning matters and not being able to see through this particular game?

A parent must remember two things when it comes to the testing of her child for a putative mental disorder. First, the pristine motivation of the mental health professional must not be taken for granted. Second, the validity of the thing for which your child is being tested must likewise not be taken for granted.

If you have your child tested to see if he has, say, "attention deficit hyperactivity disorder," it is on your shoulders to make sure that "attention deficit hyperactivity disorder" is a valid construct and that the motivation for the whole enterprise isn't suspect.

Your child can't do this for himself and the professional who is administering the test is self-interested. There is no one to cast a skeptical eye on this process but you.

Not so long ago I underwent surgery for an enlarged prostate. The enlarged prostate was real. That was no fiction. The tests run to determine the size of my enlarged prostate mattered, since one size allowed for a less invasive surgery and another size demanded a more invasive surgery. This is how real medicine works. We understand this, we respect this, and we admire this. The mental health profession uses our respect for the medical testing process to get away with creating and employing pseudo-medical tests for things that have not been proven to exist and likely exist by definition only.

As a parent, you have a simple question to ask: "You say that you are testing for ADHD. Please show me the medical evidence that ADHD exists." The *medical evidence*. Imagine a medical doctor not being able to provide you with medical evidence about the existence of heart disease, cancer, or diabetes.

I predict that in response to your legitimate question your mental health professional will either have nowhere to send you or else he or she will send you to some resource where the fabricated mental disorder is described and defined in vague, empty, non-medical language (e.g., "the mental disorder in question is a biopsychosocial kind of thing and we see a lot of it").

Without evidence that convinces you, stand skeptical. It doesn't matter that a whole apparatus for testing exists. That a test exists does not mean that the thing being tested for exists.

Before you accept that your child or teen has failed a certain test and now deserves a certain diagnostic label (with chemicals probably to follow), satisfy yourself that the diagnostic label represents something proven and real.

Imagine some little Bobby who squirms at school, squirms at church, squirms at home, squirms in his good clothes, squirms when given chores, squirms when told to sit down and chat with his aunt Rose, squirms ... a lot. What if you lived on a huge farm, it was always perpetual summer with no mandatory schooling requirements, and you didn't need to see little Bobby from morning until night? What would little Bobby be then? Would he be "ADHD"? Or would he be happy?

Wouldn't little Bobby zip in and out, make himself a sandwich, put a Band-Aid on his skinned knee, take a shower once a week or once a month, change his clothes after he fell in the pond, complain once a day about being bored, and be completely a boy? No one would be having any problems, neither little Bobby nor his parents. Where did the "ADHD" go? Where did the "mental disorder" go? Well, try to sit him down at the dinner table or in a pew at church and there it would appear again. Imagine a disease only appearing at the dinner table, at school, or in church! What sort of disease is that?

The "problem" would of course return the second you tried to impose unnatural constraints on little Bobby's energy. Try to have him sit still during a sermon in church—now you have a problem. Try to have him sit still at an authoritarian, rule-burdened dinner table—"eat your peas first, sit up straight, stop fidgeting"—and you have a problem. Try to have him not climb on something that looks promising to climb. Then you would have a problem. Have you ever seen a child NOT climb on things that were there to be climbed on? Asserting your stubborn desire to climb on everything you encounter may well get you into hot water but it should not get you a mental disorder label.

Martin Whitely on the Invention of ADHD

Martin Whitely, PhD, is a mental health advocate, researcher, and former teacher and politician. Much of Martin's focus during his 12 years as a Member of the Western Australian (WA) Parliament went into tackling what he terms the ADHD Industry.

When he was first elected in 2001 Western Australia was a world ADHD hotspot. However, after prescribing-accountability measures were tightened in 2002 there was a 50% fall in WA

ADHD per-capita prescribing rates by 2010. This coincided with a 51% fall in self-reported teenage amphetamine abuse rates in WA. Martin contends this shows that if you stop giving children a free source of amphetamines they stop abusing them.

Eric Maisel: *You are critical of the current dominant paradigm of diagnosing and treating mental disorders based on symptom pictures. Can you describe your position a bit?*

Martin Whitely: My good friend Adelaide psychiatrist Jon Jureidini calls labels like ADHD "unexplanations" because they rob understanding of an individual's personal circumstances. Jon's right; causes matter. You can't properly fix many problems without understanding what is causing them. Psychiatric diagnoses rarely involve identifying a cause and virtually never involve finding a cure.

Too often "diagnosis" means applying a dumbed-down, one-size-fits-all label to a very broad set of behaviors. In the long run, which biological psychiatry routinely ignores, treatments should match causes. The current emphasis on quick generic diagnosis matched to a drug *de jour* sometimes delivers limited short-term symptom relief but often at massive long-term cost.

I accept that for individuals exhibiting extreme psychotic symptoms it is often necessary to intervene and sometimes sedate without knowing the cause. However, I don't know anybody who has benefitted from being labeled a schizophrenic. Most of the so-called schizophrenics I know are mentally healthy most of the time. Labels like schizophrenic, pre-psychotic, and depressive rob human dignity and too often create a self-fulfilling prophecy of misery.

It is even more worrying when ordinary behaviors like losing things, fidgeting, being forgetful, being distracted, or being impulsive are turned into symptoms for concocted "disorders" like ADHD. They are not symptoms, they are behaviors; perfectly normal behaviors, especially for children. In some cases, they may require some attention, love, and/or discipline, but they don't require amphetamines.

EM: *You take a special interest in ADHD and dispute whether it is a scientifically sound, objective, or legitimate diagnostic category. Can you share your thoughts on ADHD?*

MW: Nothing demonstrates what a nonsense diagnosis ADHD is better than the now well-established late birthday effects. Four, soon to be five, large-scale international studies have established that children who are born in the later months of their school year cohort are far more likely to be labeled ADHD and drugged than their older classmates.

This late birthday effect is just as strong in Taiwan and Western Australia, where prescribing rates are relatively low, as it is in North America, the home of ADHD child drugging. That says ADHD isn't over-diagnosed or overmedicated, but that it is fiction.

Imagine if the ADHD label hadn't been invented and I suggested to you that we give amphetamines to children who frequently lose things, fidget, play too loudly, are distracted, and interrupt. You would dismiss me as either a fool or a charlatan and you would be right.

The ADHD industry has been incredibly successful because they have reversed the burden of proof. Instead of them offering compelling scientific evidence that ADHD is a neurobiological disorder, the onus has been put on poorly resourced ADHD skeptics to prove it isn't.

The ADHD industry uses half-truths to build a lie. Yes, some children are naturally more inattentive and/or impulsive than others. Yes, there is probably a genetic basis to behaviors and, yes, low-dose oral amphetamines narrow focus. But none of that makes losing your toys or fidgeting a disease.

Put plainly ADHD is BS and it is time responsible grown-ups said so. Drugging distracted kids with amphetamines and similarly dangerous drugs is disgraceful. Twenty years from now adults will look back and wonder what their parents' generation was thinking.

EM: You were also in politics and know politics from the inside. Given the reality of politics, how can the institutionalization of the current dominant mental health paradigm be effectively disputed, if it can?

MW: For most politicians, mental health is a mysterious field. Many believe we need to do something about mental health; however, very few have any concept of what needs to be done. As a consequence, they rely heavily on "experts" for advice. This is standard practice as politicians can't be expert in everything they are required to make decisions about.

The problem is that in Australia, and I suspect internationally, most of the influential, well-resourced "experts" are industry-friendly proponents of biological psychiatry. The most dangerous of them are those that talk the language of "recovery" and "prevention" but in fact promote speculative labeling and the too-early use of biochemical interventions.

A key to changing the dominant "label and drug" paradigm is confronting the disease mongers and debunking their pseudo-science. Another key is to demand from our politicians that our regulators are independent and guided by robust science. However, it is not enough just to win the debate in the scientific literature. It needs to be won in the media, both social and traditional.

So much of the excesses of biological psychiatry, excesses like ADHD and juvenile bipolar disorder, are ripe for ridicule. If you can win the popular culture debate, public opinion and therefore our political leaders, will follow. The most influential exposé of psychiatric excess in the 1970s was *One Flew Over the Cuckoo's Nest*. We need similar exposés that both entertain and educate.

Psychiatrists and other mental health professionals concerned about the direction of mental health policy and practice have a special responsibility to speak bluntly and make their profession worthy of survival. In my opinion, they need to be more willing to take on their own rogues and with less emphasis on polite discourse and more on the truth.

EM: What are your general feelings about prescribing so-called psychiatric medication to young children, youths, and adolescents?

MW: I would have no problem if medications were used for the benefit of the child alone, within scientifically justified parameters, as a short-term intervention in extreme cases where all other less invasive options have been tried. However, we are so far away from this that the best policy might be to push for a blanket ban on the use of psychotropic medications in children under a specified age.

> Even when medications are prescribed within approved guidelines, too often approval has been granted based on biased, shallow, short-term research.
>
> EM: *If you had a loved one in emotional or mental distress, what would you suggest that he or she do or try?*
>
> MW: Firstly, I hope that I would have the good sense to listen to them, hear what is distressing them, and try to respond accordingly. I don't profess to have any special expertise but I do think traumatized people are best off in familiar environments surrounded by people they know, love, and trust.
>
> In terms of seeking professional help, if I couldn't get them to see one of the psychiatrists I trust in my home town of Perth, Western Australia, my advice would be stay away from psychiatrists. In my experience of advocating for hundreds of mental health patients, a significant minority of psychiatrists are very poor listeners, who are too quick to label and too free with the prescription pad. They may only be a minority but they do enormous damage. Randomly choosing a psychiatrist is not a lottery I would want any loved one to have a ticket in.

We shouldn't label children with non-existent mental disorders. This is oppressive. It is unfortunately the case that oppression of this sort goes on all the time.

David Walker is a licensed psychologist in Seattle, Washington who's consulted with the Fourteen Tribes & Bands of the Yakama Indian Nation since 2000. Prior to moving into private practice, he was a core faculty member of the Washington School of Professional Psychology and has served on faculties at Heritage University, Oakland University, and Wayne State University Medical School. David explained to me:

Attention Deficit Hyperactivity Disorder (ADHD) is the new way to label American Indian children as "feebleminded." Tuning out and misbehaving in relation to the stultifying, manualized, test-anxiety-ridden public education system is entirely understandable, and that's where ADHD kids are often first "detected." If one looks at the social amnesia of today's mental health system, you'll soon discover that current ideas and concepts have many historical echoes. There's little attention given to the fact that newer ideas in Western mental health are often merely updated language.

For example, during the height of the American Indian boarding school era in the 1930s and 1940s, the term "feebleminded" was used to describe children considered "morally defective" as a result of being too active or impulsive, nonconformist, inattentive, or rebellious. In this way, such children were maligned and segregated from whatever limited opportunities were available to others considered to be their superiors.

When we look at today's public education system in the U.S., which has continued to fail Native children, we find the current epidemic ADHD diagnosis began in Indian Country in the late 1990s. It is only in the last 10 years that the high rate of U.S. ADHD diagnosis in other children has even begun to catch up.

The fact that Native children remain more than twice as likely to end up in special education classrooms than children from other ethnic backgrounds speaks to the continuity of historical segregation and their stigmatizing as uneducable by the U.S. mental health system. ADHD, therefore, continues a process that "feeblemindedness" began. This process was so effective by the late 1960s that surveys of emerging teachers revealed the vast majority were reluctant to teach American Indian kids. Even today, it remains difficult to recruit quality educators toward the beleaguered American Indian education system in the U.S.

Marilyn Wedge is a family therapist with 27 years of experience. She is the author of three books, most recently A Disease Called Childhood: Why ADHD Became an American Epidemic. *Dr. Wedge holds a doctorate from the University of Chicago and was a post-doctoral fellow at the Hastings Center for Bioethics. Marilyn explained to me:*

As a child therapist since 1987, I have seen an alarming increase in children being diagnosed with mental disorders and prescribed psychiatric drugs. For more than 25 years, I have helped children by using safe and effective family and school interventions. I have successfully treated all kinds of childhood problems—attention and focusing issues, school misbehavior, distractibility, anxiety, oppositional behavior, and sadness—without ever referring them for psychiatric medication.

In 1987, when I started my practice, less than 3% of American children were diagnosed with what was then called ADD. By 2016, the number increased by 300%. Today, 12% of our children are diagnosed with what is now called ADHD. Alarmed by this explosion in diagnosis, I decided to write *A Disease Called Childhood* with three purposes in mind: (1) to understand the causes of this exploding epidemic of ADHD diagnoses; (2) to discover the effects of culture and society on how children's problems are understood and treated; and (3) to offer parents practical strategies to help their children without psychiatric drugs.

When I researched ADHD in other advanced countries, I found that the rates of diagnosis have remained relatively low. In France and Finland, for example, the number is 1% or less. Unlike the United States, the typical treatment for childhood troubles in these countries is not medication, but family therapy and interventions at the child's school. Diagnosing a child takes at least eight sessions of evaluating the child and his family, not going through a 20-minute checklist of symptoms.

If ADHD were a true biological disorder of the brain, why is the rate of diagnosis so much higher in America than it is abroad? Or is it a matter of perception—of how children and childhood are viewed in various cultures? In my research, I found that differing approaches to psychiatry, parenting, child diet, electronic screen exposure, and education accounted for the difference in rates of ADHD across the globe.

Robert Berezin has practiced the long-term intensive psychotherapy of character for 45 years, taught at the Department of Psychiatry at The Cambridge Hospital, Harvard Medical School for 30 years, and is the author of Psychotherapy of Character. He explained:

This is a terrible time for parents whose children are referred to the mental health system. The last thing in the world that any child needs is to be given a mental illness diagnosis or to be told they have a mental disorder. Children may certainly have problems, but they should not be thought of in terms of mental illness. They are just kids.

In today's world of psychiatry children will almost definitely become labeled. If you are going to work with a professional, with whatever degree, it's important for them to be clear that despite some insurance diagnosis, they understand that a child's issues are not biological. Remember never use a label with a child (or an adult for that matter).

Most issues derive from family problems and school issues. Children with different temperaments will react with different kinds of symptoms. ADHD as a so-called disease is fictitious. Yes, kids get out of control behaviorally and impulsively, along with having concentration issues. This comes from a child with an active temperament who needs clear boundaries and physical activity. When they are too out of control there needs to be family therapy and behavioral therapy and the school needs to be adaptive. That's what's needed, not labeling and chemicals.

ADHD as a Linguistic Product

To say that so-called mental disorders like ADHD are fictions is to say something about how language can be used for nefarious purposes and how it in fact is being used for such purposes.

For over a hundred years, philosophers of language like Ludwig Wittgenstein and social, political, and cultural critics like George Orwell have pointed a sharp finger at the power of language to serve tyrants, persuade the gullible, and harm society and its citizens.

Here is Carl Elliott on this subject. Elliott is Professor in the Center for Bioethics at the University of Minnesota and his books include *White Coat, Black Hat: Adventures on the Dark Side of Medicine* and *Better than Well: American Medicine Meets the American Dream.*

> Eric Maisel: *Can you share your thoughts on how language helps "create" non-existing entities like "mental disorders"?*
>
> Carl Elliott: Wittgenstein has a famous thought experiment in the *Philosophical Investigations* called the beetle box game.
>
> Imagine a game [writes Wittgenstein]. Suppose everyone had a box with something in it: we call it a "beetle"—beetle here in scare quotes. No one can look into anyone else's box, and everyone says he knows what a beetle is by looking only at his beetle. Now it would be quite possible for each person to have something different in his box, Wittgenstein writes. It would even be possible for the contents of the boxes to be constantly changing. In fact, it would even be possible for all the boxes to be empty—and still the players could use the term "beetle" to talk about the contents of their boxes. There doesn't have to be any actual beetles in the boxes for the game to be played.

> What's the point here? The point is that the words that we use to describe our inner lives—words like "depression" and "anxiety" and "fulfillment"—get their meanings not by pointing to inner mental states but from the rules of the game: the social context in which they are used. They are like the word "beetle" in Wittgenstein's game. We learn how to use the words not by looking inward and naming what we find there, but by taking part in the game.
>
> The players do not all need to be experiencing the same thing in order for the words to make sense. I say I am depressed, you say you are depressed, we both understand what the other means—yet this does not mean that our inner psychic states are the same. We can all talk about our "beetles" yet all have different things in our boxes.
>
> Now this doesn't mean that psychological suffering isn't real. It's a point about the grammar of psychological language. Generally speaking, there are no independent, objective tests for mental disorders: no blood work, no imaging devices, nothing. Psychiatrists can't just open up the box and look at the beetle. The diagnoses they give to patients are determined not by what they see in the box, but by the rules of the game.
>
> And psychiatrists don't write the rules. The rules are organic, flexible, and constantly changing: new mental disorders come and go every year. Even if psychiatrists could write rules for what counts as a mental disorder, as in the DSM, they would still be indeterminate, because of the grammar of psychological experience. Everybody can have something different in his box, and still play the game.

It is vital that as a helper and/or a parent you remember that behaviors are not symptoms of a medical disorder unless they *are* symptoms of a medical disorder. We must fairly and appropriately distinguish between a behavior like restlessness, which in virtually all children is not a symptom of a medical disorder, and signs and symptoms that are indeed indicators of a medical disorder.

Should a child learn to be orderly in school? Yes, for the sake of civil society. But that is a very different question from whether a child should receive a mental disorder diagnosis for not being orderly in school. There the answer is no. The issue of "being orderly in school" is not a medical one. That little Bobby is squirming is not a reason to label him with "mental disorder," place him on the equivalent of street drugs, and set him up for a lifetime battle with addiction.

As a helper, do you explain all of this or even any of this to the mother sitting across from you who is dealing with a disruptive child, feeling guilty about her part in the problem, feeling disappointed that her child is "turning out badly," and burdened by other challenges that are causing her "presenting issue" of despair? Yes, you do and you should. You and perhaps you alone are in a position to help her think through what is going on, avoid the pitfalls of the current label-and-chemical system, and find workable solutions for an issue that is contributing to her feelings of despair.

Your client is going to be pressured from all sides into presuming that her child has a pseudo-medical condition called "attention deficit hyperactivity disorder." You may be the only person in her life in a position to help her think about what is going on in a different, truer, and more helpful way.

3

DECONSTRUCTING OPPOSITIONAL DEFIANT DISORDER

In real medicine, you use symptoms to help you discern a cause, which then helps you pick a treatment. For example, you take fever, fatigue, swelling, and so on as indicators of, say, a particular virus; you run tests to see if it is that virus; and, if it is, you then attempt to deal with that virus.

If you can't discern the cause or if you can't decide between two or more causes, you run more tests and, while you are trying to identify the cause, you do things that you know or that you suspect are likely to help relieve the symptoms. Symptom relief is a genuinely useful enterprise and you certainly engage in it in medicine; but it is not everything that you are attempting to do, not by a long shot.

In the meantime, as you seriously look for the cause, you work to reduce the pain or bring down the fever, which you do while you continue to investigate what is actually causing them. You do not focus all of your efforts on reducing the pain or on bringing down the fever. You continue your investigations. You are trying to figure out what is going on. Your job isn't merely to treat symptoms.

One of our neighbors recently suffered from terrible stomach pains. For a long time, of the order of two months, no conclusive diagnosis could be reached among the four contenders vying as the cause of her affliction. Finally, it was conclusively determined that it was cancer located in a certain stomach valve. Treatment began immediately. All along she was being given relief for her symptoms—relief for the pain, help with her inability to keep food down—while the cause was being determined. Treatment for the actual affliction could only commence once it was identified. That is how medicine works.

In the pseudo-medical specialty of "children's mental health" something very different goes on. There you take the report of a child's behavior—for example, that little Johnny pulled on the braids of the girl sitting in front of him—and for no reason that you can really justify you call that a "symptom of a mental disorder." You collect several of these "symptoms of mental disorders"—often three or four are enough—and you attach a provided label to that "symptom picture."

The label might sound like "oppositional defiant disorder" (ODD). Little interest is shown in what is causing the behavior; little interest is shown in whether the behavior reflects something biological going on, something psychological going on, or something situational going on. This is not medicine, no matter how many white coats happen to be in the room.

The Diseasing of Defiance

As a busy parent with no training in the matter, you may have only a very vague understanding of how the mental disorder industry operates. You may not really understand how the label that industry would like to affix to your defiant child has come into existence for all sorts of shadowy reasons, including the desire on the part of mental health professionals, pharmaceutical companies, researchers, and everyone else at the trough to make money. What you may understand least of all is the mental health industry's tradition of designating those who are defiant as deviant.

Is every defiant child a freedom fighter? Of course not. How absurd! Disrupting your fourth-grade class is not the same as embarking on the underground railway. Throwing a fit is not the same as standing up to King George. But is "oppositional defiant disorder" a label meant to subjugate and to serve the needs of the authorities? Yes, absolutely. It has an intention. Its intention is not therapeutic (there is zero medicine going on) and its intention is not benign. Its intention is to provide a rationale for subjugation and its goal is submission.

The proof of this is obvious enough. If I demand that you stop a behavior without inquiring into what is causing it, then all that is on my mind is that you stop the behavior. I want the behavior to stop. Period. The mental health industry's lack of curiosity about what is causing childhood outbursts is proof positive that only peace and quiet are what are wanted. Here is the Mayo Clinic on the matter of causation: "There's no known clear cause of oppositional defiant disorder." Johns Hopkins: "The cause of ODD is not known." WebMD: "The exact cause of ODD is not known." Why all this not knowing? Because an unstated goal is not trying to know what is going on, it is trying to stop what is going on.

As a parent, you may well agree with this goal. You may well just want the behavior stopped. That's completely understandable. But if you also have as your goal producing a liberty-loving, truth-telling, passionately free man or woman, you had better be careful about doing too good a job of wrestling your child into submission. You may win the battle and you may manage to crush certain unwanted, even sometimes intolerable, behaviors out of existence. But you may lose the war.

Because ODD is not typically treated with chemicals, and because chemicals make money, the following frequently happens. Your defiant child may also receive a second diagnosis, usually an ADHD or a depression diagnosis, where chemicals are prescribed routinely. Since—as with defiance—squirming, boredom, restlessness, and sadness have all been diseased, it's entirely possible that your defiant child will end up with two or three medical-sounding mental disease diagnoses and a multiple chemical fix. You may not understand exactly how this came to pass but there you are with a little patient on your hands. This came about because we have allowed putative experts to disease behaviors.

A child who loses his temper, argues with his parents, defies his parents' rules, and is spiteful and resentful is given, based on these three or four "symptoms," the pseudo-medical sounding label of "oppositional defiant disorder" and eventually put on chemicals whose job is to make him more obedient (usually via a second diagnosis like ADHD or childhood depression). This is not medicine but rather behavior control instituted to make the lives of adults easier.

Why not ask little Johnny why he is angry and resentful? Is that such a preposterous approach? Why not step back and see if his family is in chaos? Why not look at his life and not just his "symptoms"? Why presume that a child arguing with his parents is caused by some impossible-to-find medical condition? Isn't it more likely—by a thousand-fold—that he is angry with them?

We don't know why little Johnny is acting the way he is. But we do not believe it is cause-less and we do not really believe that it is the result of a medical condition. Certainly, we ought to test for genuine organic problems like brain damage or neurological damage that can cause explosive rage. But in the absence of such biological markers we are obliged to presume that little Johnny has everyday human reasons for his anger. Once you rule out brain damage and other possible biological causes of his rage, your next step should not be to posit a made-up, invisible medical condition but rather to treat little Johnny like a human being with everyday human reasons for his anger and resentment.

That Doesn't Count

One of your jobs as a parent is not to nod in agreement when something doesn't make sense to you. For example, say that your son, who throws some real tantrums and who is having school difficulties, is being evaluated by a psychiatrist. The psychiatrist asks you about the frequency and volatility of the tantrums. You reply, "They happen all the time, but only with his two older brothers." The psychiatrist replies, "Oh, those don't count."

You could nod your head in agreement, signaling that you agree that those tantrums of course wouldn't count. Or you could get suspicious and wonder, what sort of thing is a "mental disorder" if some tantrums count and others don't? You may think that I'm joking that tantrums with siblings somehow don't count enough when a child's tantrums are being added up. But that's the fact.

Here's the exact language from the DSM-5, the shopping catalogue that mental health professionals employ to provide labels. The DSM-5 defines ODD as:

> A pattern of angry/irritable mood, argumentative/defiant behavior, or vindictiveness lasting at least 6 months as evidenced by at least four symptoms from any of the following categories, and exhibited during interaction with at least one individual who is not a sibling.

If all of your child's furious outbursts are with siblings, he has no mental disorder. Add one grown-up to the mix, or one of his fellow students in class, and now you do have a mental disorder. Think about what this way of conceptualizing a mental disorder must mean. It must mean that a tantrum per se, even a zillion of them, doesn't indicate a mental disorder. If tantrums, defiant behavior, vindictiveness, irritability, and the other so-called symptoms of a mental disorder actually signaled the presence of a biological illness, disease, or disorder, then all such incidents should count in the tallying, shouldn't they?

Let me repeat this. You say to your child's psychiatrist, "All of my son's terrible tantrums are with his siblings."

"Then he doesn't have a mental disorder," he replies. "Sounds like a behavior problem."

"Oh, I forgot," you add, "once in a while he's also defiant with my husband and me."

"Ah! Now it's a mental disorder."

You could nod, since a fellow in a white coat just made a pronouncement. Or you could ask, "Please explain that to me." What could his explanation possibly sound like? Try to make one up that sounds plausible to you.

Next the psychiatrist says the following funny thing to you. "How long has this been going on?"

"About five months," you say.

"Ah," he replies, "then it's not a mental disorder yet. Come back in a month."

"But it's a real problem for us!"

"Yes, no doubt it's a real problem. But it's not a mental disorder, not until he displays the symptoms for six months."

You could nod and say, "Oh, I see. Okay." Or you could ask, "Please explain that to me." What could his explanation possibly sound like? Try to make one up that sounds plausible to you.

Next you mention the following. You say, "By the way, we come from a culture where pretty much everyone throws tantrums all the time."

"Ah," the psychiatrist murmurs, disappointed. "Then your son doesn't have a mental disorder."

"But we want him to stop his tantrums!"

"No doubt. You certainly have a problem. But if tantrums are normal in your culture, he has no mental disorder. Maybe your culture has the problem!"

Again, you could nod and say, "Oh, I see." Or you could say, "Please explain that to me. Isn't this a biological matter, this mental disorder thing? Or are you saying it's just a cultural thing?" What could his explanation possibly sound like? Try to make one up that sounds plausible to you.

Your child's tantrums are real. They constitute a genuine problem for him and for everyone involved. Let me repeat that. Your child's behaviors are real. I need to say that three or four times because you may be thinking that I am saying that the behaviors are not real or do not exist. They are real and they do exist. What I am saying is that no set of behaviors, no matter how much they disturb us, can be called a pseudo-medical-sounding mental disorder or mental disease just by adding up the behaviors and saying, "That's a lot." That's absurd and illegitimate.

The first question you must ask yourself is "What's going on?" Can that be adequately answered? Probably it can't. Who can say why *exactly* a defiant child is defiant? But as you begin to investigate the various explanations that try to account for these behaviors, you will begin to sense what *might* be going on. Is it possible that your particular reward-and-punishment system might not be working? Is

> it possible that you're looking at developmental delays that are frustrating your child? Could it be that your child's problem-solving skills are underdeveloped? Is your child playing out some family chaos or crisis? You may not be able to discern what *is* going on but you can certainly educate yourself as to what *might* be going on.
>
> The second natural question is, "Given these various possibilities, what might help?" The "might" in that question is very important. Can it make any sense to hope for an answer that comes with a guarantee? Even if you're feeling desperate and even if you can't tolerate what's going on, there is nothing you can try that could possibly come with a guarantee. But that doesn't make them not worth trying. A change in how you parent might make a huge difference. A change in family dynamics might make a huge difference. A change in how you relate to your child might make a huge difference. Efforts of this sort must be worth your time, mustn't they?
>
> It is convenient to claim that a child displaying certain behaviors has the mental disorder of ODD. That takes everyone else but the child off the hook. But to agree with that claim, you are obliged to agree that the criteria used to apply that label make sense to you. Do they? If you look at them and think about them, I doubt that they will. Then you will be thrown back on not knowing for sure what's going on with your child and be forced to try things, like changing how you deal with your child, that are effortful and that come with no guarantees of success. Doesn't that sound like the necessary, legitimate way?

One fact alone should prove the absurdity of considering these behaviors a pseudo-medical "mental disorder." Imagine for a second that I said to you that my not being able to see any symptoms of your cancer was proof that you had cancer. Or imagine that I said to you that my not being able to see a break in your bone on an X-ray was proof that you had a broken bone. You would find those assertions pretty darn odd. Isn't it fascinating that mental health service providers are warned that they may not get to witness any "oppositional" behaviors because a child with this "disorder" is likely not to demonstrate any defiance except with his parents and teachers? How strange! Does any medical condition operate that way?

Unlike in real medicine, where the sore is visible both at home and in the examining room, with the behaviors associated with "oppositional defiant disorder" those behaviors are likely only observable when little Johnny is actually angry, namely at school and at home. It is absurd but true that an indicator that you have the mental disorder of "oppositional defiant disorder" is that you do not display any signs of it when you are talking to someone with whom you don't happen to be angry. Seriously, shouldn't the fact that little Johnny is only angry around his parents suggest that little Johnny is angry with his parents?

Picture what a mental health provider is doing here. He does not personally see any signs of little Johnny's ODD and he takes not seeing them as further proof that little Johnny has an ODD. He relies on reports of things that he has not observed for himself, things that are of course more logically signs of rebellion, protest, and anger than "symptoms of a mental disorder," and from those reports he "diagnoses" a pseudo-medical condition called a "mental disorder" and moves on (usually via a second diagnosis) to dispensing chemicals. He has not seen the "disorder," he has no tests for the "disorder," and he is basing his "diagnosis" in part on the fact that he has seen nothing of the "disorder"!

This is akin to the absurd claim made that proof of the presence of an attention deficit disorder is the fact that you do not display it when something interests you. Might it not be the case that you like to pay attention to things that interest you, like sports and video games, and don't like to pay attention to things that don't interest you, like math class and your parents' dinner conversation? It is only through the looking glass that my interest in the things that interest me and that my failure to rage at someone who hasn't angered me are signs of some pseudo-medical "mental disorder."

Ten Tips for Helping an Explosive Child

Ross W. Greene, Ph.D., was on the faculty at Harvard Medical School for over 20 years, and is now Founding Director of the non-profit Lives in the Balance (www.livesinthebalance.org), on the faculty at Virginia Tech and the University of Technology in Sydney, Australia, and author of the books *The Explosive Child*, *Lost at*

School, Lost & Found, and *Raising Human Beings.* He provided me with the following ten tips for helping an explosive child.

1. Don't worry too much about obtaining a diagnosis for your child. While it might feel like a diagnosis "certifies" that there's something different about your child, diagnoses don't actually provide much information about *why* your child is oppositional and explosive. Plus, childhood psychiatric diagnoses are just labels that are applied to clusters of challenging *behaviors.* But the behaviors are just the ways in which your child is *communicating* that he or she is having difficulty meeting certain expectations. Whether your child is hitting, spitting, biting, kicking, throwing things, screaming, swearing, or destroying property, the behaviors are communicating the same thing: *I'm stuck ... there are expectations I'm having difficulty meeting.*

2. Know this: What the research that has accumulated over the past 40 to 50 years tells us is that behaviorally challenging kids are lacking certain skills, especially those related to flexibility, adaptability, frustration tolerance, and problem solving. That's why these kids explode or exhibit challenging behavior when certain specific situations are demanding those skills. The research does *not* tell us that behaviorally challenging kids are poorly motivated, so those sticker charts and time-outs may not be doing you much good.

3. Know this too: Like all of us, behaviorally challenging kids exhibit challenging behaviors *when the expectations being placed upon them outstrip their skills.* Because they're lacking skills, the clash between expectations and skills occurs more often in behaviorally challenging kids ... and their reaction tends to be more extreme. That explains why behaviorally challenging kids aren't always challenging: the clash between expectations and skills isn't constant ... it's *situational.*

4. One of the best things you can do for a behaviorally challenging kid is to figure out what skills he or she is lacking and what expectations he or she is having difficulty meeting. In my model—now called Collaborative & Proactive Solutions (CPS)—those unmet expectations are called *unsolved problems.* How do you figure those

things out? By using an instrument—don't worry, it's only one sheet of paper—called the Assessment of Lagging Skills and Unsolved Problems (ALSUP). You can find the instrument on the website of my non-profit, Lives in the Balance. And don't worry, it's free, just like all the rest of the vast array of resources you'll find on that website.

5. There's something else you'll find on that website: *how to start solving those problems with your child*. While lots of caregivers try to solve those problems unilaterally, through the imposition of solutions—that's called Plan A in the CPS model—you'll be a lot more successful if you solve those problems *collaboratively* instead (that's called Plan B). When you solve problems collaboratively with your child, you become partners—teammates—rather than enemies. You can learn all about how to solve problems collaboratively on the Lives in the Balance website.

6. If you're going to solve problems collaboratively, then you also want to solve them *proactively*. The heat of the moment is bad timing on solving problems. But how can you solve problems proactively when your child's challenging episodes are so unpredictable? Well, they're actually not as unpredictable as they might seem. Once you use the ALSUP to identify those unsolved problems, they become predictable and can be solved proactively.

7. You'll need to prioritize before you start solving problems. One of the biggest reasons the unsolved problems of behaviorally challenging kids remain unsolved is because caregivers tried solving them all at once. That a sure-fire way to ensure that none gets solved. Once you've created a comprehensive list of unsolved problems—all the expectations your child is having difficulty reliably meeting—pick two or three to work on first. The rest you're setting aside for now (that's called Plan C). Which unsolved problems should you prioritize first? Any that are causing safety issues. If there are none of those, then perhaps those that are causing challenging episodes most frequently.

8. One of the nice things about seeing your child's difficulties through the prism of lagging skills and unsolved problems is that it permits you to stop referring to your child in ways that

> are inaccurate and counterproductive: attention-seeking, manipulative, coercive, unmotivated, limit-testing, button-pushing, and so on. And while mental health professionals have often referred to the parents of behaviorally challenging kids as passive, permissive, inconsistent, non-contingent, inept disciplinarians, those characterizations are probably off the mark as well.
> 9. Give yourself and your child time to get good at Plan B together. This is a new skill for both of you. As you start to develop muscle memory for solving problems collaboratively and proactively, you'll also start to notice that your communication and relationship with your child is improving. It's all good.
> 10. Know one more thing: disagreements are inevitable. Kids having difficulty meeting expectations is inevitable. It's how you solve those problems that either causes conflict or fosters collaboration.

There are many things that we might wish for some defiant little Johnny. We wish that he were having an easier time of it. We wish that he could stop his raging, for his own sake, since he is making everyone around him dislike him. We wish we knew what was causing his difficulties so that we could offer him help at the same level as his difficulties. If he is raging because school is too difficult for him, we would offer one sort of help; if he is raging because his parents are abusive alcoholics, we would offer another sort of help; if he is raging because he can't abide his parents' strict rules, we would offer another sort of help. We wish all this for Johnny.

If a child has a medical condition, treat the medical condition. If a child is angry with his parents, do not call that a medical condition. Labeling an angry child with the pseudo-medical sounding "mental disorder" label of "oppositional defiant disorder" may serve adult needs for peace and order, just as prisons do. But it is not medicine and it is not right. Little Johnny is making it very difficult on the adults around him, who will naturally return the favor by making it hard on him. But that he is making life hard is not the same thing as him being mentally ill.

We simply must stop saying that he is suffering from a mental disorder, that is, that he has a medical or pseudo-medical condition. It makes no sense on the face of it to believe that an angry child is angry because he has a disease. It makes much more sense to believe that he is angry because he is angry, just as you are angry when you are angry. Maybe little Johnny is a lot angrier than you are—but that he is angrier than you are doesn't turn his anger into a disease.

> Dr. Bonnie Burstow is a professor in Adult Education and Community Development at the University of Toronto, a feminist psychotherapist, an antipsychiatry activist, a socially engaged philosopher, and a leading critic of psychiatry. Her books include Radical Feminist Therapy and Psychiatry and the Business of Madness. She explained:
>
> First, it is important for you as a parent to know that besides the fact that the diagnoses are hardly discrete but blend into one another, they are so broad that everyone, just by virtue of being a living human being, will meet the criteria for at least two or three psychiatric disorders.
>
> It is likewise important to know that there is not a shred of biological evidence that any of what are called "mental disorders" are even in the vague vicinity of a real disease (for information on what in regular medicine qualifies something as a disease, see my book *Psychiatry and the Business of Madness*, Chapter 2). Rather they are ways of being, of thinking, and of acting that professional others have come to pathologize, then list in their official book of disorders—the DSM.
>
> As such, despite how the professional who provided this diagnosis may think about it and/or may be encouraging you to think about it, or how any written material that he has handed you constructs it, all that you have really discovered here is that your child is a member of the human race who has happened to bump into a psychiatrist.
>
> The fact that he or she may well be experiencing severe difficulties does not alter this reality. We all have difficulties in life. Such is the nature of being alive. What compounds the problem is that there has been a huge upsurge in declaring children "mentally ill," which

> opens the door to so-called treatment (something in the interest of the industries which profit from it).
>
> None of this makes these diagnoses meaningful. Your child is not a host of a mysterious disease entity, not "schizophrenic," and not a classic case of "conduct disorder" but is the same wondrous complex kid he or she was before. Moreover, he or she is someone who can have as good a life as any, irrespective of whether or not he or she currently feels troubled or even strikes you as psychotic.

As a society, as practitioners, and as parents we may not be equipped to deal all that effectively with our sad, anxious, and angry children. But the answer to that shortcoming must not be to call them all diseased. That is not the right path or the right direction.

4

DECONSTRUCTING BIPOLAR

All psychiatric diagnoses are suspect, insofar as they are descriptive and not explanatory. To say that a person is having a "manic episode" is simply to provide a name for certain observable behaviors, for instance that she is running naked down the corridors of her dorm or staying up all night, night after night, to paint and repaint the walls.

To call these "manic episodes" is to name them without explaining them in the slightest. But with respect to mania as it manifests in adults, the name is at least intelligibly related to the behaviors we see. This is much less true for the "mania" that is supposedly a part of juvenile or pediatric bipolar disorder. There, all we might be seeing is an ordinary two-year-old rushing from activity to activity. To call that particular rushing, which is practically a defining feature of being two years old, a "symptom of the mental disorder of juvenile bipolar disorder," is not intelligible—or legitimate.

What is it that psychiatry is really trying to say when it announces that a two-year-old has juvenile bipolar disorder? Have you ever been around a two-year-old? Don't they sometimes rush from activity to activity? Don't they sometimes melt down and have ferocious tantrums? Don't they sometimes "suffer from excesses of energy"? Can't they sometimes become inconsolably sad? Aren't they sometimes willful and defiant? Yet all of these states and behaviors, as completely normal and ordinary as they are, are now deemed "symptoms of the mental disorder of juvenile bipolar disorder." Shouldn't your parent-clients be helped to understand this?

> ### Her Lost Year
>
> *Tabita Green is an author, speaker, blogger, and community organizer. She's also a mother who, with her daughter Rebecka as co-author, shared the latter's odyssey through our current mental health system in a book called* Her Lost Year: A Story of Hope and a Vision for Optimizing Children's Mental Health. *Tabita explained to me:*
>
> It all started when my daughter, Rebecka, was 13 years old. She expressed feelings of depression and also lost a significant amount of weight. She had friends with anorexia, so it was easy to jump to the conclusion that she had an eating disorder.
>
> Her pediatrician prescribed an antidepressant, which didn't feel right in my gut, but we wanted to trust the professionals. A couple of months and a medication switch later (to Prozac), she started hallucinating and became suicidal. Her pediatrician threw her hands up and recommended that we find a psychiatrist (easier said than done).
>
> Before Rebecka even had her first appointment with an outpatient psychiatrist, she had a frightening experience with her hallucinations that prompted us to admit her to a psychiatric hospital. We were at a loss as to how things could go downhill so quickly.
>
> In my experience, psychiatric medications are offered as a first, rather than last, resort. My young teen daughter saw a professional exactly once before they recommended that we "kickstart" her treatment with an antidepressant. This led to a year of hospitalizations, polypharmacy (the use of multiple drugs by a single patient), and extreme weight gain. My husband and I went along with it because we wanted to trust the professionals.

However, we didn't know then that the pharmaceutical companies peddle these drugs to physicians on an ongoing basis. We also didn't know that half of all continuing education for physicians is sponsored by drug companies. And we definitely didn't know that most of the psychiatric drugs given to children are not widely tested on children and often not even approved for use in children.

One of the biggest struggles for me and my husband was that there was never an exit strategy. When we asked our daughter's psychiatrist about it, he shrugged and said that she would probably have to be on drugs the rest of her life. That is not very encouraging, nor very conducive to healing. Medication may mask symptoms, but it doesn't help heal the underlying trauma or malnutrition or unsuitable school environment or whatever the real problems may be. In a way, medication allows us to *not* have to deal with the underlying problems.

During that ensuing year, she was hospitalized eight times and prescribed a variety of antidepressants, antipsychotics, and antianxiety medications—all the while losing her ability to function in the real world. Fortunately, a friend lent us a copy of Robert Whitaker's book, *Anatomy of an Epidemic*, which gave us confidence to ask the attending psychiatrist (Rebecka was hospitalized at the time) to stop all medications. He agreed. This was the turning point toward recovery.

> The system doesn't offer a whole lot of hope, so as parents, we must find it elsewhere. The hope comes from knowing that "mental illness" is not a brain disease. There is no evidence that a chemical imbalance in the brain *causes* mental distress. With that myth out of the way, we can start to get to the bottom of what's really going on.

To call certain childhood behaviors "manic" is to do a particular disservice to bright, sensitive, creative kids who may be restless because they're bored and under-engaged or because they have a roving curiosity that makes them play with this toy for a minute, read that book for another half-minute, and rush around from activity to activity "as if" manic or hyperactive. If your client is bright, sensitive, and creative, as she may well be to have sought out psychotherapeutic help, then her child is also likely bright, sensitive, and creative—and therefore at a much higher risk of one day receiving a juvenile bipolar disorder diagnosis.

Mania, Pressure, Creativity, and Intelligence

Bipolar used to be called manic-depression. The idea was that these "ill individuals" cycled between something called "mania" and something called "depression." But what was this thing called "mania"? No one knew—and today still no one knows.

I have a hypothesis. I take "mania" to be a state where a person's racing brain, already racing, races even faster, can race out of control, and can sometimes race right off the tracks. Mania in my view is not a medical illness but a state of pressure and a state of siege.

In my view, a person's brain begins to race because it has been set in motion for all sorts of everyday reasons and as a result of multiple pressures. Then something additional occurs, very often an existential crisis, resulting in a dangerous increase in speed. It is this added pressure on top of already existing pressure that causes the thing called mania.

I've worked with creative and performing artists as a therapist and a creativity coach for more than 30 years and their concerns interest me a lot. One of those concerns is this thing commonly called "mania." People who are creative and who think a lot are more prone to so-called mania than people who do not think a lot and who aren't creative.

This fact, which is indeed a fact, should alert us to the possibility that mania is not some pseudo-medical condition or some brain abnormality but rather a function of the mental pressures put on individuals who use their brains and who rely on their brains.

That intelligent, creative, and thoughtful people are the ones more regularly afflicted by the thing called mania is beyond question. Research shows, for example, a clear linkage between achieving top grades and "bipolar disorder" diagnoses, between scoring high on tests and "bipolar disorder" diagnoses, and between other, similar measures of mental accomplishment, brainpower, and mania.

There is plenty of evidence to support the idea that so-called mania disproportionately affects smart, creative, thoughtful people. One study involving 700,000 adults and reported in the *British Journal of Psychiatry* indicated that former straight-A students were four times more likely to be "bipolar" (or "manic-depressive") than those who had achieved lower grades. Are these folks "more ill" than their C-average counterparts or are they putting their brains under relatively more pressure, thereby causing dangerous speeding accidents? Which seems more likely to you?

In another study, individuals who scored the highest on tests for "mathematical reasoning" were at a 12-times greater risk for "contracting bipolar disorder." Similar studies underline the linkage between creativity and mania, and we have thousands of years of anecdotal evidence to support the contention that smart and creative people often get manic (just think of Virginia Woolf). Doesn't all this evidence suggest that enlisting your brain—say, to write a novel or to solve a riddle in theoretical physics—is a rather dangerous act, since it increases the pressure on a brain already pressured to deal with everyday matters like financial difficulties, psychological threats, or just finding your car keys?

"Manic-depression" and "bipolar disorder" are in quotation marks in the previous paragraphs because the current naming system used to describe "mental disorders" is weak and highly suspect. It leads to many odd, wrong-headed hypotheses, for example that "because you are bipolar you are creative" or that "perhaps mania accounts for the higher test scores." What is likely truer is that the greater a person's brain capacity and the greater a person's reliance on thinking, the greater his or her susceptibility to a brain inclined to race. If you rev up your brain so as to think long and hard, why wouldn't your brain be inclined to race?

Mania is a racing brain driven extra fast—and ultimately too fast—by added pressures, needs, or impulses. Your brain was already racing; now it is racing dangerously. Because of these added pressures, anything that gets in the way of this felt forward motion—a physical obstacle, another person's viewpoint, even a delay in the bus arriving—is viewed as a tremendous irritation. Hence the irritability so often associated with mania. This irritability makes perfect sense: if you *must* get on with whatever your dangerously racing brain is proposing—to get every wall painted red, to capture that song you're trying to compose, to solve that theorem you've been working on for six months—*then nothing must get in the way.*

It is this "must" that is at the heart of mania and that turns an everyday racing brain into one that begins to race out of control. This "must" is the heavy foot on the pedal that is driving your racing brain too fast. There is a sense of emergency here, most often an existential emergency, as you stare at nothingness and find yourself petrified by the view. You must get away from that horrible feeling and with a kind of strangled laugh that mimics mirth but that isn't mirth you turn to your brain for help; and in order to help you, protect you, and even save you, it goes into overdrive.

All of the characteristic "symptoms of mania" that we see, including (apparently) high spirits, heightened sexual appetite, high arousal levels, high energy levels, sweating, pacing, sleeplessness, and, at its severest, when the train has run off the rails, hallucinations, delusions of grandeur, suspiciousness, aggression, and wild, self-defeating plans and schemes, make perfect sense when viewed from the perspective that a powerful pressure, likely existential in nature, has supercharged a brain already feverishly racing along. Your powerful thinking machine, already running at top speed, rushes off to handle this emergency; and all the "symptoms of mania" naturally follow.

The preceding is an uncommon view of mania in adults. As to what is going on in children, we know exactly as little. But don't children already have racing brains, a feverish fantasy life, imaginary playmates, wild schemes, and all too often trauma-induced "mind pressures"? Doesn't it make sense to conceptualize "mania" in children, when it is really something different from normal childhood curiosity and distractibility, as related to the way the mind can be pressured, in children as well as adults, to race too wildly? If it is ever fair to call a child "manic," isn't this the direction in which we should look?

Diagnosing children with juvenile or pediatric bipolar disorder is largely an American phenomenon. Do we have more "bipolar children" in the United States or are we simply labeling more of our children?

The labeling of American children with so-called mania and so-called depression has risen dramatically in the last 20 years. If the "mania" part of "juvenile bipolar" is a problematic construct, so also is the "depression" part. Might not any of the following cause the thing commonly called "depression"?

- A child gets a string of bad grades and begins to feel hopeless about his chances at school.
- A child is being bullied by a sibling, learns over time that he can't come to his parents with his complaints or his pain, and feels helpless in his own home.
- A child grows up scrutinized at every turn by a stay-at-home parent who expects nothing less than perfection.
- A child is forced to live in a chaotic environment filled with marital discord, broken promises, and a lack of privacy.
- A child begins to see life as unfair and a cheat and sours on life itself.
- A child receives no permission to do any of the things that he or she actually enjoys doing and lives a life of rules and chores.
- A child has his or her efforts criticized and ridiculed in cruel and shaming ways.

There are countless possible non-medical, non-biological reasons for a child's despair. But despite this obvious truth, your parent-clients must be helped to understand this. They have been trained to ignore the obvious, that life can cause serious sadness, just as you've been trained to believe that you are "diagnosing mental disorders" when in fact you are affixing labels to "symptom pictures." By helping them get clear, you are also staying clear yourself.

It really isn't very honest to use "depression" as a pseudo-medical word to collect all sorts of states and behaviors, like boredom, recklessness, irritability, alcohol abuse, and anger. To say that a child is "depressed" when he is actually and obviously irritable and angry is to make a linguistic leap that is exactly as illegitimate as saying that you are "depressed" when you are in fact irritable and angry.

Nor should the word be used as a twisted repeating of a self-report. It shouldn't work the following way, where a child says, "I'm depressed," meaning something along the lines of "I'm being bullied" or "I hate life," and his psychiatrist repeats, "You're depressed," but with a completely different, now pseudo-medical, meaning associated with the word. What just happened is that the child's everyday usage of the word got repeated with a sly twist, turning the child's sadness into the "mental disorder of depression."

> ### "Depression" Must Exist, Mustn't It?
>
> Most people, even if they do not feel that they really understand what "mania" connotes, intuitively feel that they do know what "depression" connotes. They have what they consider the common-sense belief that the mental disorder of depression exists. Why do they believe this? For the following 15 reasons.
>
> 1. *There is a culture-wide acceptance that "depression" is a "mental disorder." Isn't this culture-wide acceptance, approaching worldwide acceptance, proof of its existence?*
>
> No. There is certainly a phenomenon. But for the phenomenon to be a disease or a disorder, it must be a disease or a disorder. That something needs remediating or changing doesn't make it a disease or a disorder. The fundamental linguistic game played by the mental health industry is to characterize anything that even remotely needs remediating or changing a "disorder." That hundreds of millions of people agree to play this game is only proof of the power of naming.
>
> 2. *We see "depression" everywhere. It is epidemic. Isn't the fact that we see it everywhere and that so many people are suffering from it proof of its existence?*
>
> No. What we see are a great many unhappy people, some mildly unhappy and some profoundly unhappy, who have naively or pointedly adopted the language of the mental health industry and who are willing or eager to characterize their unhappiness as this

thing called a "mental disorder." What we see is a great deal of unhappiness. We do not see "depression" anywhere unless we play the mental health industry's naming game.

3. Since mental health professionals say that such a disorder exists, mustn't it exist?

No. Mental health professionals once said that women who didn't want to be subjugated by their husbands were hysterical. Just a few short years ago mental health professionals said that homosexuality was a mental disorder. Mental disorders come into existence by virtue of a handful of people in a room deciding that a phenomenon ought to be called a mental disorder. Once this naming occurs and is codified, the rest of the profession goes along with the naming and the general population follows. A group of people sitting in a room and deciding that certain human phenomena ought to be designated a mental disorder doesn't make those phenomena a mental disorder.

4. Isn't the fact that countless books, articles, websites, and guests on talk shows say that such a disorder exists proof that it exists?

No. Virtually all people who use the word "depression," whether in connection with their own depression or the depression of others, have not investigated whether the phenomenon they are talking about is more properly thought of as a "mental disorder" or as profound unhappiness. They are simply parroting words and constructs provided by the mental health industry. That countless people use a word isn't proof that the word means what the creators of the word say that it does. It only means that the word has become the shorthand—and in this case incorrect and inappropriate—label for a phenomenon.

5. Isn't the fact that countless people assert that they know what unhappiness feels like, that they know what depression feels like, and that they are certain that the two are completely different things, proof that depression is a mental disorder?

No. They are certainly experiencing one state as different from another state. One correspondent who wrote me expressed the difference this way: "Whereas sadness makes you feel raw and skinless, depression is like wearing a snow suit and mittens and wondering why you can't feel the caress of life." However, that something feels worse than something else or different from something else isn't proof that it's a "mental disorder." Riding a rollercoaster feels very different from rocking on your porch but the former isn't a "disorder" just because it turns your stomach and makes you scream.

6. *Since drugs exist for its treatment, doesn't it make sense to presume that it's a medical condition?*

No. Chemicals have effects. That a certain chemical has a certain effect isn't the slightest proof that it is "treating" a "disorder." Imagine a rampaging elephant loose in a village. You can down it with a tranquilizer dart but does that mean that you've "treated" its "rampaging disorder"? No. You simply used a chemical to produce an effect.

7. *Since it is treatable, mustn't it follow that it is some sort of medical condition?*

No. The word "treatment" as used by the mental health industry is part of a naming game and has neither a medical nor a common-sense meaning. With regard to "mental disorders," "treatment" doesn't mean "the helpful things you do after you have accurately identified the causes of a problem." A medical doctor treating an illness orders this treatment versus that treatment based on his understanding of what is causing the illness or his hypothesis about what might be causing it. A mental health professional asserts without blushing or blinking an eye that he has no clue as to what is causing your "disorder" but that he is nevertheless happy to "treat" it. This is an illegitimate use of the word "treatment" and would never pass muster in any other hospital examination room.

8. *Mustn't there be all sorts of scientific evidence that there is a mental disorder called depression?*

No. Nor can there be, because first you would need a definition of "mental disorder" that was not specious. What scientific evidence could prove that your boredom, say, was a "mental disorder"? That some part of your brain didn't light up when you were bored? That some hormone got secreted when you were bored? That some neural transmitter functioned in some unusual way when you were bored? *All of that would only be evidence that you are bored, not proof of a mental disorder.* It is impossible to find scientific evidence to prove that a certain common human experience is a "mental disorder" unless you engage in fraudulent science.

9. Since medical tests are sometimes ordered, mustn't it follow that doctors are looking for the causes of a real disorder or verification of the existence of a real disorder?

No. Medical tests like blood tests are not used to diagnose "depression." Rather, they are used to identify or to eliminate from consideration organic problems (e.g. central nervous system tumors, head traumas, multiple sclerosis, syphilis, hypothyroidism, or various cancers) known to cause the symptoms of depression or to exacerbate the symptoms of depression. For example, if you were to present insomnia as a symptom, there are tests to run to see if the insomnia might be related to some organic problem. Running this sort of test is not the same thing as "testing for depression."

10. Since there is compelling evidence that the brain actually changes its shape when a person is severely depressed and that parts of it can even atrophy, isn't that proof that depression is a mental disorder?

No. Let's say that you sit on your couch for a few months straight. You would expect to feel weaker. Would you call that weakness a disorder or would you call it the natural result of sitting on your couch for a few months straight? That a body part begins to weaken and atrophy from a lack of use should be credited to its lack of use, not to a disorder. The fact that there is an observable biological event doesn't prove—or even imply—the presence of a disorder.

11. Maybe "depression" isn't a "biological disorder" but don't we have ample proof of the existence of a "psychological disorder" called "depression"?

No. What would constitute a "psychological disorder"? First, you would need a definition of "psychological disorder" that wasn't specious. Such a definition would need to do more than assert that certain unwanted experiences, grouped together, amounted to an illness. Second, you would need sensible ways of distinguishing between normal human experience and whatever it is you'd defined as a "psychological disorder." Third, you would need to mount treatments that addressed the causes you identified and not just the symptoms. None of that currently happens—nor could it ever legitimately happen as long as the thing being pathologized is ordinary human experience.

12. Because psychological tests can distinguish between "depressed people" and people who aren't depressed, doesn't that prove that the "mental disorder" of "depression" exists?

No. A psychological test asks you questions about your life experiences that you then answer. In essence, a psychological test is a certain kind of self-report. You might, for example, indicate that you were sleeping poorly, that life held little interest for you, and that you were overeating. Then the game would be on: the more you painted a picture of unhappiness, the more you would get a "high depression score." Self-reports can certainly distinguish between happier and unhappier people. But to say that you have "tested for depression" is completely false.

13. If your circumstances improve and you don't feel less depressed, or if nothing in particular is going wrong and you still feel depressed, doesn't that prove that what you're experiencing must be a disorder?

No. You can be unhappy even though your circumstances are excellent. You can be unhappy even if nothing in particular is going wrong. You can grow unhappy just because a cloud passed across the sun and you were reminded of your own mortality. To grow unhappy even though "objectively" all is well isn't proof of a disorder. It is only a completely understandable feature of human existence. Unhappiness can arise even at the moment when you feel happiest as you catch a whiff of nothingness or lament that this happiness is bound to prove fleeting. It is no proof of a "mental disorder" called "depression" that you might feel unhappy even though the sun is shining.

14. If what I'm experiencing isn't a mental disorder, shouldn't I be able to just cheer up or buck up?

No. Your unhappiness may be pernicious. Your unhappiness may have many causes. You may view life through a lens that turns everything gray. That it may be *possible* to "cheer up" or "buck up" is very different from supposing that it should only take a snap of your fingers to realize it. And what is that "should" supposed to connote anyway? There is no one on the face of the earth who can arbitrate your happiness or unhappiness. That you can't easily improve your mood or that you have no interest in improving your mood proves nothing about your mood being a "mental disorder" called "depression."

15. Well, but something is going on, isn't it?

Yes. Of course, *something* is going on. A lot of human unhappiness is going on. That *something* is going on isn't proof of the existence of a "mental disorder" called "depression." Maybe you want to hand off the problem of your unhappiness to the putative experts. That desire is understandable. Maybe it embarrasses you to admit that you're profoundly unhappy when you can't see how your unhappiness is justified by your circumstances. That embarrassment is understandable. Maybe you find it hard to admit that life has turned out to be a cheat. That reluctance is understandable. Maybe you have all sorts of reasons for preferring to believe that your unhappiness is a "mental disorder" called "depression." All those pressing and poignant reasons notwithstanding, your unhappiness is not "the mental disorder of depression."

Your parent-client needs your help in understanding that the construct of juvenile bipolar disorder is extremely shaky and suspicious. With some children, nothing but childhood is going on. With others, something is indeed going on, but to presume that the something that is going on is pseudo-medical in nature is unsupported by any scientific evidence. ADHD, ODD, juvenile bipolar disorder, and the other constructs of psychiatry are not rooted in science or medicine. They are labels affixed to a troublesome child or a child in trouble. The trouble is real and genuine: but what is going on is nothing like a broken arm in need of casting.

5

MEDICATION OR CHEMICALS?

If the so-called mental disorders of childhood like ADHD, ODD, and juvenile bipolar disorder are not actual medical matters, why are the children who are receiving these diagnoses being put on so-called medication?

First, because that is the current system, one that is highly profitable for the parties involved. Second, because giving someone a pill for something regularly produces a positive placebo effect. Third, these so-called medications, because they are powerful chemicals, have powerful effects, some of which may sometimes be wanted or may seem to be warranted.

In the future, if we are wise enough to look this distinction in the eye, we will begin to understand the difference between chemicals-with-effects and medications that treat illnesses. Currently we are not that wise. We carelessly call a chemical a drug even if it is not treating a disorder or a disease. By so doing we play right into the hands of the mental health establishment: into the hands of folks who want us to think that the chemicals-with-effects that they wantonly prescribe are legitimate medicine. These so-called medications are surely chemicals-with-powerful-effects, effects that may indeed be wanted sometimes. But they are not medication employed for the treatment of actual medical issues.

Interview with Brent Robbins

Dr. Robbins is Chair of the Department of Humanities & Human Sciences, Associate Professor of Psychology, and Chair of the Graduate Council at Point Park University in Pittsburgh, PA. He has a Ph.D. in Clinical Psychology from Duquesne University. He is a Past President of Society for Humanistic Psychology, Division 32 of the American Psychological Association. He explained in an interview:

> Eric Maisel: *You are the co-editor of* Drugging Our Children: How Profiteers are Pushing Antipsychotics on Our Youngest and What We Can Do to Stop It. *Can you give us the headlines of your findings and conclusions?*
>
> Brent Robbins: The book is looking specifically at the overuse of antipsychotic drugs with young people, but it also speaks to a broader concern with the fact that child psychiatry, and psychiatry in general, has been driven by market forces more than medical research.
> The book examines the scientific evidence, and finds that there does not seem to be an empirical justification for prescribing antipsychotic medications to children; in fact, on the contrary, there are many reasons why many alternative treatments should be considered first, not least of all because of the very high risk of side effects from this class of medications. For example, children placed on antipsychotic drugs are put at higher risk of potentially irreversible motor disorders, obesity, and diabetes, to name a few. In addition, we do not fully understand the long-term consequences of these drugs, and there is a compelling body of evidence that suggests these drugs might more likely produce long-term disability rather than prevent it.

> Despite the research evidence that should dissuade physicians from prescribing antipsychotics for treatment of children, we have seen shockingly high increases in the prescription of these medications both in children and for treatment of the elderly. We show how these trends are driven primarily by the massive marketing dollars invested by the pharmaceutical companies who manufacture these drugs.
>
> The book also contains a legal argument from an attorney, Jim Gottstein, who argues that clinicians who encounter children on these medications have an ethical responsibility to inform the parents and/or guardians of the risks of these medications. Clinicians who are not medical doctors can recommend that the parents seek a second opinion, and refer the parents to someone with expertise in children's issues. The clinician might consider a referral to an M.D. who may be able to offer alternative, safer treatments.
>
> Finally, the book outlines and describes alternative treatments for children that have demonstrated effectiveness in addressing the kind of problem-behaviors that are increasingly targeted with anti-psychotics. The implication is that non-medical, alternative treatments, that are free of medical side effects, should be, at the very least, attempted prior to considering more invasive medical interventions.

Medicine is wonderful. But the chemicals employed to "treat mental disorders" are not medicine. Not every chemical used by a person to create an effect can rightly be called medicine. If we use language this loosely and call every chemical with a powerful effect a medicine then we have completely bastardized language and made a mockery of the ideas of disease and of medication. Biologically altering our experience of life via chemicals is not the same as treating illnesses with drugs. If we are not adamant in our defense of this distinction then every single chemical compound is raised by loose language to the special status of medication.

Human beings have used chemicals to alter their experience of life since the beginning of time. Peyote, magic mushrooms, Scotch, marijuana, cocaine, nicotine, caffeine, heroin, red wine: the list of chemicals used by human beings for the purpose of feeling different is very long. It is only metaphoric—and a profoundly dangerous and ill-chosen metaphor—to call these "medications that treat the disease of life." You can call these chemicals sacred, dangerous, a blessing, a problem, or whatever else you like: only don't call them medicine.

A chemical becomes medicine in context. It *changes its name by virtue of how it is being used*. The chemicals called antibiotics are being used to treat your infection. They are still "mere" chemicals but they have been legitimately elevated to the high status of medication by virtue of why and how they are being used. We call them medicine because they are being used to treat an actual disease. If the disease were not there—if we were not using these chemicals to fight something worse than the chemicals themselves—we would not subject anyone to those powerful chemicals.

Certain problems conspire to make our conversations about mental health and medication so problematic. First is the completely loose way that we use the word "drug." It would help us tremendously if we reserved the word "drug" or "medication" or "medicine" for those times when we used a certain chemical to treat a particular ailment, malady, injury, disorder, or disease. In order to use the word "drug" or "medication" there would need to be a direct relationship between the chemical and the disorder. Only then would the chemical rise to the status of "medicine." Two things would be required: that there is a disorder and that the chemical *directly* affects it.

If there is no disorder to treat, you can't call the chemical you take "medicine." Just as it would be useful to reserve the word "drug" or "medication" or "medicine" for those times that a chemical was used to treat an actual disorder, it would be useful not to make up disorders that do not exist. Cancer is one thing and "communism as a cancer of the mind" is another thing. The first is a medical condition; the second is a metaphor. If you drink vodka to get over your enthusiasm for communism, in that transaction vodka is not "medication" and your enthusiasm for communism is not "a mental disorder." Vodka is not medication and can't be medication in this instance, not because it is a mere chemical but *because* there is no disorder present except metaphorically.

Marijuana is a substance. It is a mere chemical-with-effects when we smoke it to alter our experience of reality and it is medicine if we smoke it as treatment for our glaucoma. Glaucoma is a certain identifiable medical condition and not a metaphor. "Life sucks" is a certain existential or psychological issue, real in its pain but not a medical condition. Smoking marijuana to "leave life for a bit" is not a "treatment" of anything medical but rather a characteristic use of a certain chemical substance to alter our experience of reality. If we could reserve "drug," "medication," or "medicine" as words that we only use when we are talking about treating actual biological disorders that would amount to a giant step forward.

Jo Ann Cook is the author of *Making Healthy Children Sick: What the Mental Health Industry Is Not Telling You*. She explained:

In 2009, after working for 20 years as a social work consultant in the special education department of a large metropolitan school board in Canada, I was advised at a staff meeting that approximately 20% of children and youth were suffering from mental health problems. I was skeptical. Our school board had never previously referred to students in these terms.

At the time, I was concerned about the increasing use of behavior-altering and mind-altering psychiatric drugs in children and adolescents within the school system. Ritalin and other ADHD drugs began to surface in the 1990s, followed by antidepressants and antipsychotic drugs in the early 2000s.

Teachers widely promoted these medications and claimed that they helped students do better socially and academically. These beliefs were completely at odds with long-established theories on the stages of normal child development, the importance of social factors in both behavior and educational outcomes, and the results of independent pediatric clinical trials which showed there were more harms than benefits.

Now, I was told that the government supported drugging children. Yes, the government. The government not only mandated "mental health" training for all teachers and administrative staff but developed comprehensive action plans and targets to identify students who were suspected of having mental disorders, and directed school professionals and teachers to connect these students to community mental health services, such as pediatricians and hospital psychiatrists. It was an unconscionable act against vulnerable children.

My day-to-day involvement with students at all levels and ongoing examination of their school progress in classrooms, report cards, psychological reports, and medical reports, clearly demonstrated that students who were medicated with psychiatric drugs often developed disturbing behaviors and explosive outbursts, which lead to disability and school failure. My complaints to professional associations and local and federal politicians fell on deaf ears.

This indefensible trend was accepted by the majority of community health professionals and physicians, who readily endorsed these medical practices. They justified the practice of using harmful drugs on children, as scientifically based necessities, and helped to organize walk-in clinics and other programs to persuade parents that their children needed psychiatric services and pharmaceutical products.

Independent clinical trials, free of drug company influence, have repeatedly shown that psychiatric medications are ineffective, unsafe, and harmful to developing brains and bodies; and can cause severe anxiety, disturbed thinking, aggression, metabolic disturbances, suicidal thoughts and behaviors, even death. These risks are never disclosed to the public. They don't sell drugs.

Consider Jordan, a grade 10 student, who was referred to his school's professional support team for non-attendance issues. His story of injury is just one of many among the millions of children, who are told that they are sick and need medication by the adults and professionals, who have the responsibility to protect children from harm.

His school records indicated that Jordan, at the age of four, was a bright and independent child. He was from a loving two-parent family. Upon entering kindergarten in 2001, his teachers observed that he was precocious, but willful and challenging, in terms of limits placed on his behavior, behaviors that are normal in many parts of the world.

The school advised Jordan's parents to seek a medical assessment. A community psychologist reported that Jordan was indeed bright but he would benefit from a clear, consistent structure. There was no sign that Jordan was anything other than a normal, healthy child at this time.

By grade 3, Jordan was reportedly having difficulty managing class routines. He seemed overly concerned with getting the correct answer and often refused to complete his work. The school again asked his parents to get an assessment from a doctor.

It was now early 2006, and there had been a dramatic change in the way that community professionals and doctors viewed childhood behaviors. A local hospital clinic promoted the view that 13% of children and youth were suffering from anxiety disorders, with more girls receiving the diagnosis. The normal fears of children were transformed from a normal, developmental stage to a mental disorder needing medication.

A second psychological assessment at age eight reported Jordan was very bright, almost gifted, but appeared to be fearful of making mistakes. The parents were encouraged to help Jordan use positive coping statements. The psychologist persuaded Jordan's parents to agree to a referral from the family's doctor to a mood/anxiety clinic at a nearby hospital, believing that medication might benefit Jordan.

In 2008, after a medical assessment at a mood/anxiety clinic, Jordan, now ten, was prescribed Prozac by a psychiatrist, who was considered to be an expert in mood disorders in children. Instead of getting better, Jordan's behavior deteriorated dramatically. He became aggressive, easily angered, was considered a danger to others, and made significant threats to his parents and siblings.

At age 12, he was hospitalized in a youth psychiatric unit for four weeks after threatening to kill himself and acting aggressively toward family members. The unit psychiatrist diagnosed Jordan with generalized anxiety disorder and Asperger's disorder. He was prescribed two new medications, Celexa, an antidepressant, and Risperdal, an antipsychotic drug and released. He was then monitored by his family physician as an outpatient.

> Industry supporters would like to believe that the medical treatment that Jordan received led to successful academic outcomes and a hopeful future. This did not happen. He became extremely fearful, withdrawn, and did not want to attend school. In grade nine, he attended 20% of the time. By grade ten he was no longer attending school.

You may be among the vast majority of helpers who are in no position to know whether psychiatric medications are really medicine or whether they are chemicals-with-powerful-effects being used illegitimately and wantonly as putative treatment for so-called mental disorders.

You may likewise find yourself among the vast majority of helpers who are in no position to monitor the psychiatric medications that your client's child may be on, in no position to make concrete or specific recommendations about the use or the cessation of those chemicals, in no position to argue for withdrawal or to suggest how that withdrawal ought to proceed, and in no position to take an unequivocal stand for or against the use of such chemicals.

What you *are* in a position to do is to make it clear to your client that these matters are controversial, that the mainstream view is not the only view, and that it is incumbent upon her to educate herself about these controversies. There are plenty of places to point her. One such place is Joanna Moncrieff's *The Myth of the Chemical Cure*. Joanna, a Senior Lecturer at University College London and a consultant psychiatrist in the NHS in London, explained:

> There is an assumption that the drugs prescribed for mental health problems work by targeting and reversing an underlying chemical imbalance (or some other brain abnormality). What I wanted to tell people in *The Myth of the Chemical Cure* is that there is no evidence that this is the case, and that there is an alternative way of understanding what drugs do which is much more plausible. I called these two ideas the "disease-centered" and "drug-centered" model of drug action. The disease-centered model is the idea that the drugs target an underlying disease or abnormality; the drug-centered model is the idea that drugs exert psychoactive (or mind-altering) effects in everyone regardless of whether or not they have a psychiatric diagnosis.

For example, antipsychotic drugs dampen down thinking processes and emotions because they have a generalized inhibiting effect on the nervous system. This is what appears to reduce psychotic symptoms, not the targeted reversal of underlying chemical imbalances. I go on to demonstrate the lack of evidence for the disease-centered model for every major class of psychiatric medication, including antipsychotics, antidepressants, "mood stabilizers," and stimulants.

Wouldn't knowing about and considering the implications of this distinction serve your client? Likewise, wouldn't it be valuable if your parent-client understood the tremendous power of the placebo effect? Let's say that I'm a school-age child and I'm obliged to take so-called medication for a so-called mental disorder. It is fascinating that whether or not my behavior actually changes by virtue of the strong chemicals I am forced to ingest, you, whether you are my parent or my teacher, are likely to feel very relieved that I am "being helped" by taking that "medication."

If asked, you are likely to report that I am much improved. It doesn't matter if the chemicals I am given are inert and part of a placebo effect experiment. You will still report that I am much improved. My taking something has eased your concerns, and you now see me differently, as a good boy on meds. Isn't this a lovely marriage of the placebo effect and the halo effect? I am much the better boy by virtue of taking something that is in fact a placebo.

The child psychiatrist Scott Shannon is director of the Wholeness Center in Fort Collins, Colorado, a collaborative care and integrative medicine wellness center, and the author of *Mental Health for the Whole Child* and *Parenting the Whole Child*. He explained:

> One of the most interesting facets of ADHD is the placebo effect. Children with ADHD typically express little placebo effect as they hold little expectation about the intended response. It appears, however, that there is a placebo effect in medicated kids' parents. A meta-analysis confirms it. Parents and teachers express a placebo effect when children are given stimulants, because the adults hold a clear expectation for the medication's effects ... Parents and teachers evaluate a child more positively if they believe that the

child has been medicated. They also tend to attribute positive changes to the medication even when no medications have been given ... This finding diminishes the reliability of parent and teacher reports in evaluating kids for ADHD—the core of the diagnostic process.

> I introduced you to Bonnie Burstow, author of *Psychiatry and the Business of Madness*, in an earlier chapter. She explained:
>
> Maybe you've been told that your child ought to go on one or more than one psychiatric medication for his or her diagnosed mental disorder or mental illness. Such advice is so routine as to be "knee-jerk" and I would suggest regarding it as inherently problematic.
>
> Correspondingly, I would alert you to the fact that just as the psychiatric diagnoses have no validity, neither do the drugs. For example, despite claims to the contrary—and the pharmaceutical companies with whom these claims originate are operating out of vested interests—the drugs are not specific to the "conditions" that they allegedly "treat."
>
> Moreover, they have been proven to do far more harm than good. Correspondingly, as opposed to addressing chemical imbalances—and there is no proof that people so labeled *actually have chemical imbalances*—quite the opposite, they create imbalances. They also impair thinking and feeling. They are particularly harmful to children for the child's brain is still in the process of developing.
>
> Now you might be tempted to accept this as a reasonable tradeoff as long as these substances help with emotional distress. While they potentially can, what you need to be aware of here is that your child can get far better help without incurring damage. Additionally, the so-called help is intimately linked with the damage caused, and beyond that is enormously limited.
>
> What relates to this is that, in effectiveness studies, it has been shown that such drugs do not even outperform innocuous substances like antihistamines. Moreover, despite claims to the contrary, they

MEDICATION OR CHEMICALS?

> themselves *cause* emotional problems—and of such huge proportion that whole countries have taken action against them.
>
> In the UK, for example, a high percentage of the antidepressants have been officially banned for use with children under 18 because suicide has been shown to be a "side effect." By the same token, it has been shown that the stimulants (the drugs routinely prescribed to children diagnosed with attention deficit disorder) cause mania and suicidal impulses. Moreover, they stunt growth.
>
> Now, I am aware that while most parents have qualms about the drugs, the average parent worries about letting their child down if they do not follow "the doctor's orders." That's quite understandable. However, your child's safety is dependent on moving beyond this default mode.

Would you buy that the word "medicine" has been appropriately used in any of the following cases? From a killer: "Arsenic is the medicine I use to treat the disease of being alive from which my victims regularly suffer." From a safari guide: "Tranquilizer darts are the medicine I use to treat the animals I encounter who are suffering from the disease of wanting to eat me." From a bar patron: "Scotch is the medicine I use to treat my disease of having a wife I can't stand." Would you accept any of those usages?

If a mental health establishment worker makes no effort to identify the cause of a child's suffering—if he is completely indifferent as to whether the child is suffering from a life problem, from a feature of her formed personality, from a feature of her original personality, from a reaction to her circumstances, etc.—if he makes zero effort and simply says, "We call this symptom picture a mental disorder and medicate it," that utterance should be received with as much disdain as you receive the utterances of the poisoner, the safari guide, and the bar patron.

Here are some questions that your parent-client might ask of a prescribing physician who would like to prescribe chemicals to his or her child. These are not the only questions your client might want to ask but they are suggestive of the *sorts* of questions he or she might want to put on the table:

1. Does my child have a medical problem? If so, what is it?
2. If it is a medical problem, are there medical tests to test for it?
3. If there are no medical tests to test for it, how do you know my child has a medical problem?
4. Why are you considering my child's behavior a symptom of an organic problem? Aren't there other possible reasons for his or her behavior?
5. If there are other possible reasons for his or her behavior, why aren't you exploring them?
6. Why are you considering my child's mood a symptom of a medical problem? Aren't there other possible reasons for his or her mood?
7. If there are other possible reasons for his or her mood, why aren't you exploring them?
8. Why are you considering my child's anxiety a symptom of a medical problem? Aren't there other possible reasons for his or her anxiety?
9. If there are other possible reasons for his or her anxiety, why aren't you exploring them?
10. My child is younger than his classmates. Isn't that relevant in deciding whether his or her behaviors merit a mental disorder label and medication?
11. My child has always been energetic and bouncing off walls. Isn't that relevant in deciding whether his or her behaviors merit a mental disorder label and medication?
12. My mate and I are going through a messy divorce. Isn't that relevant in deciding whether my child's behaviors merit a mental disorder label and medication?

Your parent-client will have to decide if she prefers to call these chemicals-with-powerful-effects "medication," in effect agreeing that something medical is going on, or whether she prefers to call them "chemicals-with-powerful-effects," in effect demanding that it be proven to her that something medical is going on. It is her choice as to how she will think about this matter. And it is your choice as to whether you want to facilitate such a conversation.

What about Stopping?

There are a multitude of opinions, controversies, and complexities around whether or not to ever provide so-called psychiatric medication to children and, if those chemicals are provided, how, when, and whether the child in question can get off those chemicals. Here are the thoughts of Sami Timimi, whom we met in an earlier chapter. Sami explained:

From my perspective both as a parent and as a professional with a thorough knowledge of the outcome literature on the use of psychiatric medication in under-18s, I would never agree to a child of mine going on any psychiatric medication apart from in extreme circumstances (for example experiencing voices telling them to kill themselves) and then only for a limited period of time until other interventions can help.

The research is quite clear in my opinion—there is very little evidence that any form of psychiatric medication used long term leads to lasting positive outcomes and much evidence that they can result in considerable harms. There is some evidence that used judiciously short term (a few days, weeks, or months) it can be beneficial. There is no credible evidence that any of the diagnoses we use are the result of biological abnormalities like a "chemical imbalance"—none has been found and therefore there are no biological tests to find such abnormalities before psychiatric mediations are given (unlike the case with most other medications).

However, as a psychiatrist dealing with struggling and worried families and young people I am also aware that many people are understandably keen to try pharmacological approaches when they feel (whether this is objectively true or not) that they have tried all that they can or perhaps having heard of others for whom they believe it was successful. If they wish us to go down the route of trying a psychiatric medication, then I suggest the best way to view them is as enhanced placebos that function primarily as "enablers." The placebo response for psychiatric medications is higher than for any other class of medications and is the main basis for any effectiveness.

> I believe that whenever psychiatric medication is used with anyone under 18, it should be accompanied by a clear plan for withdrawal of medication, typically after about six months if successful changes have taken place, but within a few weeks if there has been no positive change. If withdrawing medication after six months or longer, it should be done as a carefully phased decrease over two to three months or longer, as all psychiatric medications may result in withdrawal symptoms on stopping.
>
> In fact, it is very dangerous to abruptly stop psychiatric medication. If you do decide you would like to wean your child off psychiatric medication that they have been on long term, then I advise to do this slowly with step-wise reductions and allowing things to stabilize before reducing again. Typically, this would mean reducing the dose once a month in small steps.
>
> Hopefully your physician will support you in this, but remember, many physicians have been trained to believe that they are treating a chemical imbalance and that the child should remain on medications, so you may have to politely disagree with this. Unless your child is on a mandatory treatment order legally, then exercise your rights to decide what is right for your child; I believe most physicians will respect this and hopefully provide the relevant prescription.

To the extent that mental orders are created fictions that take painful or unwanted human phenomena and label them by committee as one thing or another, exactly to that extent must so-called psychiatric medication be called chemicals-with-powerful-effects and not medicine.

If you don't believe in the legitimacy of the current labeling system, you should also not believe in a labeling system that elevates a given chemical to the high status of medicine. In a more enlightened future, these chemicals, and more like them that are no doubt coming, might still be available and might prove helpful to some people. They just won't be called medicine, their logic would become completely exposed, and new, better conversations about their use or their avoidance would prove possible.

6

THINKING ABOUT CAUSES

If your parent-client is dealing with a child in distress who has received a mental disorder diagnosis or who looks to fit the "criteria" for a mental disorder diagnosis, then it is likely that that's the way your client will be thinking about the situation. He or she is likely to say things like "My son has been diagnosed with ADHD" or "my daughter is very OCD" or "They say my son is bipolar." Your client will naturally be thinking this way, given that this is now an everyday way of speaking.

This sort of shorthand, which appears to make it easy for all concerned to conceptualize what's going on and to come up with appropriate solutions, in fact avoids taking the time and making the effort to actually understand the situation. To understand what is actually going on, a parent or helper is obliged to consider 20 separate factors, factors that we'll examine in a moment, which is an overwhelming number and which in practical terms is virtually an impossibility to consider. What parent is equal to saying, "Let me look at Jimmy through 20 different lenses"?

To make the matter even more daunting, looking through a given lens in no way guarantees that you or your client will see anything particularly clearly. We are talking about impossible-to-know matters like the way her child organizes his inner reality, the exact nature of any new or chronic stressors in his life, the contours of his original personality, the presence of any psychological conflicts (like, for example, loving to perform but being made anxious by performing), matters of idiosyncratic gene expression, problems caused by diet, toxins, or other environmental factors, or actual medical conditions. To say that one should view matters through these many lenses is not the same as saying that one is likely to see all that much.

To make matters more daunting still, some of these lenses demand that the parent look in the mirror at his or her contributions to the problem, at the contributions of his or her mate and their other children, at the quality of their parenting skills, and at such basic matters as whether they love, respect, and care for their child. These are areas bound to bring up defensiveness, denial, shame, guilt, anger at you for pointing a finger, and a raft of negativity and resistance. If, to take one example, your client's mate is a bully (and it's likely that in as many as a quarter of all families at least one parent is an authoritarian personality), how likely is it that she is going to want to look at that directly or credit that with affecting her distressed child? Not very.

Taken together, these 20 factors are an overwhelming number. Furthermore, looking at them comes with no guarantee that much will be learned and the almost certain guarantee that your client will be upset by being scrutinized. Are these perhaps reasons to skip this sort of investigating? No. You owe it both to the child and to your parent-client to bring these matters to her attention. You might even provide your client with a handout that explains these 20 lenses and say, "The point of this handout is to provide you with a bigger picture of what's going on with Jimmy than 'Jimmy has ADHD.' If you get a moment, take a look at it and think about it a bit." At the very least, being aware of these 20 lenses will prevent you from adopting a too-easy view of "the mental disorders of childhood."

Here are the 20 lenses we're considering. I'll describe them as if I were talking directly to parents, so that, if you choose to, you can present them to your parent-clients for their consideration.

1 The Lens of Original Personality

Every child comes into the world already somebody, with his or her own temperament, endowments, sensitivities, genetic blueprint, and everything else human. He may be your child but he is already his own person, someone willful, needy, greedy, curious, loving, and patently himself. How can he be somebody else and why should he be somebody else?

If he is not well-equipped to deal with the world because of some birth reality, whether that's a particular sensitivity, a particular genetic expression, a birth defect, some large deviation from the norm in mental or physical functioning, or even something objectively positive like high energy (which becomes a negative in a world that wants him quieter and better behaved), then you will need to help him deal with that reality. But in whatever way he comes into the world, he is already someone: not an "average" someone or a "normal" someone but exactly and precisely himself.

2 The Lens of Formed Personality

Who he is "originally" starts to be altered by life. If you stress a child, even if he comes into the world sturdy, you can start to harm him and make him feel defeated. His experiences can begin to create "depression," "anxiety," "behavior problems," and all the rest, which then are not add-ons but integral features of his forming and now-formed personality. He doesn't "have depression," as if that were something to have, he is becoming or has become a depressed person, someone who looks at the world negatively and pessimistically and is "down on life."

You can help your child "form" in healthier rather than unhealthier ways by virtue of the love you lavish on him, by virtue of the quality of your parenting skills, by virtue of the sense of safety and secure attachment that you provide, and in all the other ways that amount to good, loving, thoughtful parenting. At the same time, your child's formed personality begins to harden—that's what "formed" means in this context—and he becomes more entrenched and less amenable to change. Good parenting is an excellent thing but even the best parenting is no match for the reality of an already formed personality.

3 The Lens of Mind Space

Your child has a room or a shared room where he sleeps, reads, plays video games, and all the rest. But what about that other room where he *really* resides, the room that is his mind? He takes that room with him everywhere, to school, to the playground, to aunt Rose's house, to the dinner table; and that interior room has a certain look, feel, and smell to it, just as his literal room does. He dwells in his room; he indwells in the room that is his mind; and it is the quality of that indwelling that determines his emotional wellbeing.

Human beings don't just have thoughts. They engage in all sorts of activities with names like contemplation, problem-solving, daydreaming, obsessing, plotting, musing, and calculating. Everyone does this, children included. Picture your child. You tell him that there's something he mustn't do. You watch him carefully and you see that he's calculating and deciding. It may only take him a split second to complete that calculating and deciding but some intensely human and immensely complicated operation occurs in that split second. He has a kind of conversation with himself, all in that split second, the outcome of which is that he will or won't cooperate with you. That calculating and deciding happened in "the room that is his mind," with its particular atmosphere and its idiosyncratic fittings and furnishings.

You can do a better job of picturing and understanding your child's mind if you take the time to picture and understand your own mind. If you do this work, you'll find yourself less surprised and less flustered by your child's attitudes, moods, behaviors, and personality. Rather than supposing that little Johnny or little Mary has contracted a mental disorder when he or she exhibits certain behaviors or moods, you'll be more inclined to wonder about the quality and content of his or her indwelling—and what you can do to improve your child's mental environment.

4 The Lens of Development

To yell at a small child for doing something that small children do is a bit of mean-spiritedness. Not to take the idea of "development" into account is not to treat your child fairly. If your angry toddler bites another child in a fit of pique, that is not a symptom of a mental disorder. That is something that perfectly healthy, normal toddlers will do sometimes. Yes, behaviors of that sort require parental intervention. But intervening is not the same as mistaking a behavior for a symptom of something.

Every human being is at a particular age and stage. You do not have the same interests, capabilities, and desires at 20 and at 90. If your child is younger than his classmates, he may also be less mature than them and more likely to ignore teacher commands. Is a child "out of control" expressing his formed personality, dealing with some particular stressor, or displaying a feature of natural development? These are the imponderable questions that parents face; but allowing for the possibility that development is at play is a must.

5 The Lens of Biology

Everything human is biological. That goes without saying. But we tend to think of a fractured leg as "more biological" than a regret, a missing chromosome as "more biological" than a missed homework assignment, a problem with a neurotransmitter as "more biological" than a problem with one's sister or brother. That is, in the context of childhood distress we tend to associate the word "biological" with something broken, out of whack, not functioning, and so on. This is often what parents are thinking when they see their child doing something troublesome, appearing in distress, and especially if they have to deal with a child displaying what are called "the symptoms of serious mental illness" like auditory or visual hallucinations.

While it is natural to think this way, that "something must be broken," there is rarely any actual proof that the thing a parent is witnessing *is* biological in this "something must be malfunctioning" sense. It must be the case that biology ought to be factored in, but how? The mental health industry is not particularly honest on this score, acting as if they know the biological causes of certain childhood phenomena when in fact they don't. So how exactly is a parent to think about this?

The best way may be, when confronted by something that "looks biological" in your child's emotional or behavioral life, to: get a complete medical workup for your child, hopefully from a pediatrician not invested in the current mental disorder paradigm who understands childhood and who is reluctant to label; to consider any findings, results, or recommendations you receive with some healthy skepticism; to wonder aloud about any non-medical alternatives to the psychiatric meds that may be recommended; and to research alternatives yourself.

6 The Lens of Family

Family therapy is premised on the belief that a child's distress is virtually always a function of family dynamics. These dynamics can include physical abuse, sexual abuse, verbal abuse, neglect, sparring parents, alcoholic parents, despairing parents, bullying siblings, shaming dynamics, zealotry, and intrusiveness. The list of possible adverse childhood experiences and childhood traumas is very long. But family dynamics do not have to rise to the level of trauma to be negatively affecting your child. Relatively small matters, like one child being treated marginally better than another child, can create outsized effects.

Family dynamics are within your power to investigate. Unlike many of these other possible causes, which are by their nature invisible, family dynamics are patently visible. You can take a good stab at figuring out which of your family rules don't serve the family very well. You can identify stressors that you and other family members may be piling on your child. You can tease out any unspoken expectations, mixed messages, or unfair punishments. All of that is there for you to explore and investigate.

7 The Lens of Behavior

Behaviors are complicated manifestations of our human nature. Take the "simple" behavior of refusing to eat the piece of bread in front of you, even though you are hungry. Why would anyone do that? Yet every parent has had her child refuse that piece of bread for any number of reasons, because he wants the strawberries first, because his piece of bread is slightly smaller than the piece his sister got, because this piece of bread is different from the piece of bread that he had yesterday, which he wants again, because he angry with you for making him wash his hands first, and so on. He is hungry; there is a piece of bread; he won't eat. How frustrating for you! And how human of him.

It's absurd not to connect up behavior with something human going on. Adults, too, will refuse to eat that piece of bread: because their religion tells them to fast; because the bread was presented to them on the wrong plate, violating their religion's dietary rules; because they are despondent and have no appetite; and so on. For child and adult alike, you ought not to take that "not eating a perfectly good piece of bread" as some sort of symptom of an oppositional defiant disorder or some other concocted disorder. With any human behavior, your child's behavior included, we want to understand it, not cavalierly and inaccurately label it. With respect to your child's behaviors, you might want as one of your mantras, "I wonder what's going on?"

8 The Lens of Social Connection

Even though we may enjoy and prize our solitude, prefer our own company, and have reasons to mistrust and be wary of others, we are also social creatures. Even if your child looks to need nothing except his room and his video games, he is still a social creature with needs for love, intimacy, friendship, and connection. He has other social needs as well: a desire for social mastery, a longing to win at competitions, the hope that he "looks good" and "isn't a loser," and other charged hopes and feelings that play themselves out in the social arena.

If something is troubling your child—if he wants to stay home from school, if he acts particularly irritable, if he grows despondent—it is wise to wonder if something is going on in his social world. Did something humiliating happen at school? Is his best friend no longer talking to him? Did he get rejected from the group or clique he hoped to join? Of course, your child is likely to be close-mouthed on this score and offer up nothing by way of explanation. But you can keep your eyes and ears open and wonder whether some putative "symptom" of something is actually a feature of your child's perhaps troubled social life.

9 The Lens of Experience

Your child has experiences. Those experiences matter. If something is troubling your child, isn't it reasonable to suppose that his or her feelings are connected to some recent (or remote) experience? Wouldn't you find yourself in a mood if you were just fired or if you found out that your mate was cheating on you? Aren't our experiences tremendously important with respect to our thoughts, our feelings, our moods, our motivations, and just about everything? It must be the same with your child, mustn't it?

Experiences live on in the body, often as physical ailments and complaints. Your child's headaches or stomachaches may be more related to some recent experience, some past experiences, or some pending experience than to anything purely biological in nature. Check with your child and see. He or she may not be able to make the connection or identify what's really going on, but expressing your concern in this way opens the door for some potentially helpful, healing conversations. Without being intrusive or overly watchful, do be aware of your child's experiences: they indubitably matter.

10 The Lens of Endowment

An endowment like high creativity or high intelligence is no simple blessing. With high creativity and high intelligence come restlessness, feelings of difference and alienation, a more brooding sort of indwelling ripe with obsessions, a vulnerability to addictions stemming from large appetites and excessive energy, and openings to phenomena with names like "mania" and "existential depression." I've worked with creative and performing artists for the past 30 years and I know that these predictable challenges exist right alongside the "blessing" of endowment.

If your child is bored, thwarted in his ability to use his intelligence or his creativity, ridiculed for his intellectual or creative pursuits, or is in some other way in conflict because of his natural endowments, those conflicts can play out as sadness, anxiety, obsessiveness, tantrums, irritability, restlessness, and other moods and behaviors that are likely to be pathologized in our current mental disorder environment. When your child is in distress or acting out, it's a good idea to wonder, "Is what's going on possibly related to my child's natural endowments?"

11 The Lens of Stress

Stress comes in many forms. That our boss is making demands on us is an external stressor; that we take those demands home and continue to obsess about them is an internal stressor. That we haven't enough money to pay our bills is a negative stress (or "distress"); that we have a thrilling performance upcoming is sometimes called a positive stress (or "eustress"). Stress produces stress hormones that physically weaken the body, tax the mind, and open the door for serious illness.

Children, too, are under stress. The very way your family operates may be stressing your child, if your child has to live in fear of severe punishments, is regularly blamed and shamed, can't get any privacy or respect for his personhood, and so on. School is its own stressor, especially if a child is pressured into believing that his whole future depends on how well he does in second grade. Then there are the stressors of piano recitals, kid cliques, and a hundred other everyday stressors. If your child is troubled or is engaging in troubling behaviors, doesn't it make sense to try to figure out what may be stressing him? And then endeavoring to reduce that stress?

12 The Lens of Trauma

It is arguable—and many practitioners and researchers believe this to be the case—that trauma in a child's life is the single best predictor of emotional and behavioral difficulties, including often very severe ones like lifelong despair, repetition compulsions, high anxiety, low self-esteem, addictive tendencies, and work and relationship failures.

If your child seems suddenly not himself, it makes sense to wonder if something traumatic has occurred. Maybe he is being bullied and humiliated at school; maybe a sexual predator has made advances; maybe he has engaged in some activity that feels seriously shameful or heinous. Because talking about traumatic events in one's life is notoriously difficult, your child may not be able to let you know what has transpired or what is still going on. But inquiring as to whether something bad has happened opens the door to communication and lets your child know that you care.

13 The Lens of Emotion

It's a cliché that children have feelings too. But, of course they do. Ever known a child not to experience some hurt feelings? Emotions are deep and serious matters. If your child loves something—a pet, a blanket, a toy—that love is real and even monumental. If you take that toy or blanket away, or if that pet dies, why wouldn't your child grow despondent? To call that sadness a "symptom of a mental disorder" flies in the face of what we know to be undeniably true, that human beings, children included, experience real, deep, intense emotions.

If your child is experiencing an emotion like sadness, credit it with being caused in some human way. That sadness isn't an invasion of some sort, as if your child woke up with a mood flu. He is experiencing a painful emotion. The simple questions to ask are "What's going on?" or "What's the matter?" or "What's troubling you?" Of course, your child may not have the answer or may not want to answer. But asking such a question lets him know that you recognize the simple, human reality of emotions, to which neither you nor he are immune.

14 The Lens of Circumstance

Changed circumstances matter. Your toddler can go in her diaper whenever she pleases, but after potty training accidents can occur, and with them embarrassments and even humiliations. When your child starts walking to school by himself or riding the bus by himself, a whole new world of experiences—and dangers—commence. If your children must share a room and aren't getting along, if your child goes off to summer camp and has a difficult experience, if your children start ferrying between two households because you've gotten divorced—all of that matters. Circumstances matter.

If your child exhibits a new, unwanted behavior or falls into a new, distressed mood, it's logical to ask yourself, "What in her circumstances has changed?" Maybe something only small has changed—small to you. That small change may loom gigantic in your child's life and psyche. Check in with her and ask. It may be that giving away that rambunctious kitty didn't affect you much, given that you have three other pets, but to your young daughter it may matter tremendously. It can't hurt to check.

15 The Lens of Psychology

Each of us, children included, are psychological creatures. We are not just acted upon; we are not mechanical creatures who are programmed in a certain way and then play out our instructions. Rather we are complicated creatures who experience life in a dynamic, interactive way. The best way to name this dynamism and this interactivity is to call it *psychological subjectivity*. Human life is a series of psychological experiences; a human being is a creature completely caught up in her own idiosyncratic, subjective, ever-changing personal reality.

Human beings obsess. Human beings experience internal conflicts. Human beings get envious and jealous. Human beings experience disappointment, regret, guilt, shame, and sadness. Human beings plot their revenge. Human beings feel defeated and give up. Human beings crave this and are repulsed by that, decide that this is important and that that is pointless, lose hope and regain hope. All of these are examples of our psychological nature and reality.

Your child is a psychological creature. He must be credited with an inner reality that either fully determines or goes a long way toward determining what he thinks, how he behaves, and who he is. His psychological reality can even override his instincts, causing him, for example, to rush toward danger when his body knows to run away from it. Billions of words have been written about our psychological nature and yet it is still all-too-easy for a parent to forget that her child is not just "behaving" or "misbehaving," but is rather expressing his psychological reality. An awful lot is going on *inside* your child. That must be considered.

16 The Lens of Culture and Society

If your child is gay, it makes an enormous difference whether your culture and your society consider that a mental disorder, a crime, a sin, or a natural difference to be respected. Being gay in one part of the country is a very different experience from being gay in another part of the country. Being gay in a strict religious family is a very different experience from being gay in a progressive, secular family. Your child's moods, behaviors, and very sense of self are bound to be affected by, and sometimes determined by, what his society and culture condemn, censure, license, and applaud.

Our culture and society can make us despair. Our culture and society can make us anxious. These powerful factors include everything from how drinking is viewed in the family, to how displaying affection is viewed in the community, to how anti-authoritarianism is viewed in the wider society. As with so many of these possible causes of distress, you may have no clue as to which societal or cultural factors are negatively affecting your child. But you can keep your eyes and ears open and you do possess clues, don't you? To begin with, you might try asking and answering the following question: "Might the culture and society my child is growing up in give him some trouble?" See what you come up with.

17 The Lens of Environment

We do not know the extent to which toxins, pollens, and other environmental factors of that sort negatively affect the mental health of children (and adults). Also included in the idea of "environmental factors" are diet, stress, the relationship between stress and gene expression, the effects of poverty, lack of opportunity, dangerous neighborhoods and schools, other socioeconomic factors, and such matters as living with long, dark winters. "Environmental factors" is a phrase used to cover a vast multitude of possible distressing factors in a person's life.

Given the vast multitude of environmental factors, some of which get great publicity for a moment (like the effects of power lines, cellphones, polluted drinking water, ambient radioactivity, lead paint, or toxic canals) but most of which are not on our radar at all, how can you possibly know what is affecting your child's mental health? You can't, really. But you can hold the awareness that some environmental factor might be implicated and credit environmental factors as possible culprits.

18 The Lens of Ingestion

Does your child behave the same way before and after eating all the Halloween candy he's collected? Isn't he "normal" before and wired or somnambulant after? You might take his wired state as a sign of hyperactivity or his lethargic state as a sign of childhood depression unless you knew that he had just ingested a month's worth of sugar. Because you know that fact, you aren't inclined to pathologize his behaviors.

Processed foods, fatty foods, fried foods—we do not know all the ins and outs of how diet and emotional health are connected but it makes simple sense that if your child regularly behaves in a certain disruptive way after eating a certain food, why wouldn't you make a dietary change there? That's a simple enough safety precaution; and if the behavior vanishes, that would strongly suggest that the food was indeed the culprit.

> ### Environmental Stressors and Dietary Factors
>
> Sometimes what is distressing a given child is some environmental, dietary, or chemical factor affecting his or her body chemistry. It is not fair to say that this is always the case and it is also not fair to say that this is never the case. You want your parent-client to be alert to this possibility, without overselling the likelihood that this is what's primarily or exclusively going on.
>
> What sort of body chemistry stressors are we talking about? Toxins in the environment. Smog and other air quality issues. Poor diet. Food allergies. Other allergies, like pollen. Medications, including psychiatric ones. Anything that a child ingests or comes into contact with that has the potential to alter his or her body chemistry also has the potential to negatively affect his or her mood, behavior, and overall emotional health.
>
> Sharna Olfman, author of *The Science and Pseudoscience of Children's Mental Health*, explained to me in an interview:
>
> > Two of the world's leading environmental scientists, Philip Landrigan and Phillipe Grandjean, have identified 1,000 neurotoxins, that are either used in or are by-products of industry, that pose a direct threat to the developing brains of fetuses and young children. Several of these toxins have proven links to symptoms associated with ADHD, autism, and learning disabilities.
> >
> > Diets that are deficient in micronutrients (vitamins and minerals) essential for optimal brain development have also been linked to children's psychological disturbances. This research underscores the importance of healthy diet and nutritional supplements for maintaining optimal mental health.

Epigenetics—the latest iteration in the field of genetics—informs us that environments can alter gene expression. In consequence, the hunt for the "bad" gene is now considered 20th-century science. An example of an epigenetic process that is directly relevant to children's mental health is that exposure to high levels of stress during fetal and infant development can epigenetically alter regions of the brain that help us to cope with anxiety and impulse control.

Research on the enteric nervous system (the neurons that innervate the digestive system) and its accompanying microbiome has revolutionized research on autism, as has functional neurology with its emphasis on the importance of synchrony among different regions of the brain (imagine an orchestra in which all the musicians are playing well but the first violinist is playing a half tempo slower than the other musicians). These areas of research will help solve the mystery of the explosive increase in autism diagnoses and pave the way for effective approaches to treatment.

Parents need to be reassured about the power of loving relationships, good nutrition, and time spent away from screens and out of doors. They need to be educated about the consequences of exposures to ubiquitous developmental neurotoxins such as pesticides in food, fluoride in water, pthalates in plastic, and Bisphenol A in cans, to name but a few. While parents can address some of these issues independently, with the support of therapists and/or holistic health care professionals, some of the solutions must be top down. Our government must give our regulatory bodies, the Food and Drug Administration and the Environmental Protection Agency, the autonomy they need to keep children safe from neurotoxic chemicals, and pay more than lip service to improving public policies. We must take proactive measures to keep our children healthy, rather than stemming the tide of an epidemic of childhood mental illness.

It will never be easy to know what is actually affecting a child. Is a given child's behavior issues related to his poor diet or is it more related to the fact that his family is in poverty, chaos, and upheaval, one consequence of which is a poor diet? Is it the diet or the chaos? Is it even fair to say that something like a poor diet is very often or even sometimes a contributory factor? The authors of the article "The Relationship Between Diet and Mental Health in Children and Adolescents: A Systematic Review" (in the *American Journal of Public Health*) carried out an extensive meta-analysis of research in this area and reached the following conclusions:

> Of those studies examining dietary patterns as the exposure, the majority of studies ($n = 4$) consistently demonstrated significant relationships between unhealthy dietary patterns and poorer mental health. Evidence of an association between healthy dietary patterns and better mental health was less consistent, with significant positive associations observed in only half of the 6 studies. Of the 5 studies exploring the association between diet quality, measured using diet quality scores, and mental health, all demonstrated a significant relationship between higher diet quality (i.e., higher intakes of healthy, nutrient-dense foods) and better mental health. Of the 3 studies that looked specifically at the association between lower diet quality (i.e., higher intake of unhealthy foods) and poorer mental health outcomes, 2 also reported significant relationships.

So, the answer looks to be a guarded yes. Kelly Dorfman, author of *Cure Your Child with Food: The Hidden Connection Between Nutrition and Childhood Ailments*, explained:

> There is chemistry to mood and thinking. Many parents overlook the importance of diet in mental health. A recent study found, for example, that children who are picky eaters are more likely to have depression and anxiety symptoms. Robust research over decades points to inflammation as a factor in depression, anxiety, bipolar disorder and post-traumatic stress disorder. Therapy with specific forms of long-chain fatty acids has shown promise as safe and effective treatment for these disorders. Your body is not the government and cannot operate in a deficit state. There is no place to borrow from if you are not eating what you need in order to think clearly. Diet and targeted nutrition therapy may help.

> How important are environmental factors, including diet? Many of the claims regarding the connection between these factors and mental health must be considered speculative. Some, just as with the claims of traditional psychiatry regarding the efficacy of chemical interventions, look to be downright suspect. But sometimes, maybe even more than sometimes, there may well be a causal connection between your child's environment, including what he or she ingests, and his or her moods and behaviors.

19 The Lens of Medication

A special form of ingestion are the medications your child may be taking, including psychiatric medications (or, more properly, chemicals-with-powerful-effects). Any medication your child is taking may have a placebo effect, an actual main effect, mild side effects, major side effects (including the risk of suicidal ideation), and gateway effects (priming your child for an addiction).

If your child is on psychiatric medications and his condition worsens, you do not want to blithely accept the idea that "your child needs a second medication to help with the first medication" or "we just have the dosage a little off." You want to consider the possibility that the chemicals your child is taking are themselves worsening his condition. This is an area where you must educate yourself.

20 The Lens of Life Purpose and Meaning

Your child has been over-excited about and obsessed with a present he knows is coming; he gets it; and he loses interest in it in two seconds flat, almost as soon as he unwraps it. This is an excellent example of how meaning comes and goes, even in the lives of children. Children, like adults, experience meaning, lose meaning, deem this important and that not important, and begin on their lifelong journey of arriving at their life purposes and their reasons for living.

Does your child already have a budding sense of her life purposes? She may well. She may have the inchoate sense that her dance class and her gymnastics class are really important to her; and if you suddenly decide to curtail those classes she may fall into a state of despondency that looks all out of proportion to the "mere" canceling of some extracurricular activities. Your child's moods and behaviors are intimately connected to her budding sense of her life purposes; and if she is thwarted with regard to those life purposes, there will be emotional repercussions.

***

To repeat the main headlines of this chapter, this is all too much for either you or your parent-client to consider, but it nevertheless may pay huge dividends for both of you to at least acquaint yourselves with this list. Even just a passing acquaintance may help prevent any too-easy labeling of your parent-client's child and may point her in some interesting, valuable directions.

7

CONTEMPORARY APPROACHES

Let's say that you have a parent-client who's worried that her teenage daughter has what your client is characterizing as school problems, depression, high anxiety, or some other challenge. She wants to know if she should send her child to a psychiatrist and get her diagnosed and on medication. You might want to explain the following to her: that psychiatrists differ greatly, some relying almost exclusively on diagnosing and medicating, and others relying much less so; and that there are alternatives to psychiatry, including but not limited to psychotherapy.

In this chapter I want to introduce you to some psychiatrists who do not limit themselves to diagnosing and medicating, as well as to other practitioners who operate from a non-medical model. They are provided here to arm you with ways of thinking about what you might want to say to your parent-client who is looking for help for her child. You have the opportunity to broaden your client's perspective, after which, naturally enough, your client will have to do her own research and her own thinking on the matter.

Psychiatry and Mindfulness

Russell Razzaque is a psychiatrist based in London and also a mindfulness teacher. He is engaged in research into more mindful ways of providing mental healthcare and is currently leading a national transformation project around Open Dialogue in the UK. He is also a writer and his latest book exploring spirituality and mental health is entitled Breaking Down is Waking Up. *Russell explained:*

Mindfulness and the traditional way psychiatry is practiced are really more divergent than anything else. Psychiatry is about removing emotional pain, whereas mindfulness teaches us the value of being present with our pain.

It was through the practice of mindfulness that I started to learn this new perspective and started to relate to my own pain differently. Instead of running away from it, I was taught to welcome it, to befriend it, and thus convert it into a source for my own emotional and spiritual growth. As I conducted my own development this way, I realized that there must be a different way to do psychiatry too.

That's when I really started to think about different approaches. Approaches that, while they may involve taking action—even using medication—to help people with the worst aspects of emotional pain, had the ultimate aim of helping people be with their pain as much as possible (and so rely on other treatments less).

This was the way, I realized, that long-term healing could be brought about, instead of consigning so many people to the label of "chronic."

A whole new world of possibilities thus opened up, in which psychiatry could become more than just an exercise in pain removal (though it's never really removed because it always comes back), but more fundamentally a way in which people can experience and thus grow through their pain. In order to do this, however, it would mean the psychiatrist being more able to sit with their own pain first, and so the first challenge was in teaching mindfulness to mental health professionals. From this desire, the College of Mindfulness Clinicians was born and now we run retreats every year for health professionals, with excellent attendance and even better results.

I don't think that the current paradigm has no place or validity. For some people, seeing their experience in those terms and accepting treatment in traditional medical ways is what they want and how they feel comfortable. But if we insist that this is the only way things must be understood and the only way we can help people, then we are really going to end up harming a great many people whose own creativity, background, and life experience mean that they can understand their issues in a very different way.

It's really the person having the experience who is the expert and so the clinician's role should be to help them express what they (and their loved ones) really believe deep down inside is going on, and then find their own pathway to healing through that. This way the experience becomes one of empowerment, rather than one that fosters a dependence on an "expert." For this reason, I only like to use medication as a last resort and if the client really wants it. And I'd be very wary of using such measures with young children.

Spiritual Psychiatry

Dr. Anna Yusim, author of Fulfilled, *is a practicing psychiatrist who completed her undergraduate education at Stanford University and attended Yale Medical School and the NYU Residency Training Program in Psychiatry. She has published over 60 academic articles, book chapters, scientific abstracts, and book reviews on various topics in psychiatry. She can be reached at www.annayusim.com. She explained:*

Relative to my colleagues in the field of psychiatry, I work with my patients in a unique and unusual way. In my own life and in my work with over 1,000 patients in my private practice in New York City, I learned something very important about the healing process: a complete healing requires a spiritual outcome as well as a clinical outcome.

I seek much more than bringing my patients "into remission" and temporarily alleviating their pain and suffering. What I seek is a complete healing for each and every one of my patients. While I learned a great deal about the healing process through my training at Stanford University, Yale Medical School, and the NYU Psychiatry Training Program, this important lesson was never taught in medical school or residency.

In addition to being a psychiatrist, I am also a deeply spiritual person and incorporate principles of spirituality into my psychiatric practice. Seeing oneself as connected to something greater than oneself, a loving energy that always has our back, is a very powerful tool for healing, guidance, and transformation. It is the tool that has helped me to change my life and a tool I employ to help my patients change theirs. In this way, I stand at the interface of two often-contradictory worlds: the world of science and the world of spirit.

Some of my patients are atheists and/or have no interest in spiritual principles, which I certainly respect. Others find these principles a source of guidance and a new way of seeing the world; the principles resonate with them. This work with patients is not meant to evangelize or preach a specific religious or spiritual philosophy. In contrast, it appeals to the spirit within all of us, the divine soul that is our birthright and our greatest source of guidance once we know how to access it. In my work with patients, I have found that integrating the Western medical approach with a spiritual approach is important for complete healing.

Our soul is the blueprint we bring into this world of how we are meant to grow, change, evolve, transform, and meaningfully contribute to humankind over the course of our lives. It is what some call our "divine essence," that which connects us to something greater than ourselves and, at the same time, to the deepest part of who we are and to each other. Once we learn to hear our soul's whispers and uncover its deepest longings, it will guide us to a life of meaning and fulfillment.

In my initial evaluations with patients, I am looking for their souls to emerge. I want to understand why they have come to see me at this point in their lives, on this very day, under these very circumstances. I seek to genuinely understand what is troubling my patients on the most basic existential and human level. I want to know their deepest desires and greatest fears, what makes them laugh, what makes them cry, what bores them to tears, and what keeps them awake at night. I want to know what they would be doing with their lives if nothing stood in their way and the world was their oyster. Usually, the world is their oyster; they just don't know it yet.

A disconnection from one's soul may present in many ways: anxiety, depression, obsessions, excessive worrying, suicidal thoughts, self-harm behaviors, psychosis, mania, addictions, and phobias, among many other presentations I may see in my medical office.

In many cases, although medications can treat the symptoms resulting from a disconnection from one's soul, they rarely treat the underlying etiology, which is the disconnection itself. Only by looking inside oneself and aligning with the deepest part of yourself can you address the root cause of the problem instead of the effect.

In my medical practice, only about half of the patients I treat are on medication, which is a low percentage for a psychiatrist. For certain patients, however, medications are a lifeline without which they feel they could not survive. Soul work is hard to do, even impossible, if you are so depressed that you cannot get out of bed, or so sleep-deprived from insomnia that you can barely function, or so anxious that you cannot leave the house, or in an opiate withdrawal so painful that you don't know if you will even survive the day. Engaging in soul work is necessary for complete healing, but it is predicated on first being able to function in this world. When clinically indicated, psychiatric medications can sometimes be the very tools that allow one to emerge from the darkness.

Relational Psychotherapy

Jed Diamond is a leader in the emerging field of Gender-Specific Medicine and Men's Health. For more than 40 years he has advocated an expanded understanding of physical, emotional, and spiritual health that goes beyond the current medical model. His most recent book is My Distant Dad: Healing the Family Father Wound. *Jed explained:*

For me, the term "psychotherapy" is limiting. It implies that we work with mind and emotions, but that excludes the body and pays scant attention to the spirit, soul, and broader environmental issues. When someone comes to me seeking help I want to learn everything I can about them. I'm interested in the physical, emotional, interpersonal, social, sexual, economic, and spiritual aspects of their well-being. I want to know about their hopes and dreams as well as their stresses, fears, and challenges.

We all grow up and face challenges from stresses within the family and in the larger community. Just as many emotional wounds can occur in the family constellation, the core of healing occurs in a healthy parent-child bond, along with the support of wise elders in the surrounding community. Psychotherapy can be helpful in creating a healing bond between people based on mutual trust and emotional support.

There are many types of training and theoretical orientations in modern psychotherapy. When we go beyond the differing theoretical approaches to recognize the origins of psychotherapy in the parent-child bond and the wisdom of elders in the community, we recognize that the help that clients receive is based on the core competencies of the therapist, including the following:

- All humans are works in progress. To be alive and to be human means that we have all experienced wounds and we are all in the process of change and growth.
- We are not "sick, crazy, or broken." We are perfect, just the way we are. We all do the best we can to deal with the challenges in our lives. Our ways may be difficult or troublesome to others, but there is nothing essentially wrong with us.
- The relationship is best when it is real and authentic. Therapists don't have all the answers. We are humans with our own excesses and deficits. We can be most helpful when we're being ourselves and sharing our challenges and victories.
- Healing and growth occur for both the "client" and the "therapist." In many ways, we're both the therapist and the client. One of us may be getting paid for the session, but if the therapeutic relationship is working, then both of us are healing, learning, and becoming better human beings.

When people come to me for help, they often are in a crisis and feel afraid and unsure of themselves. In some ways, they feel that their world is out of control and dangerous and that they are in danger of drowning. I have an image of the person as flailing around in a panic, feeling they are about to get sucked under the water and drown.

But what I know, that they don't know, is that the water is only three feet deep and that when they calm down they will be able to feel the bottom and know that they aren't going under. It may take months or years before their panic goes away, but I hold them in my loving embrace from the very first moment, assured that they are fine, just the way they are.

Group Psychotherapy

Susan Raeburn, Ph.D. is a licensed clinical psychologist in Oakland, California with over 25 years of experience doing individual and group psychotherapy. She has been a staff psychologist at Stanford University Medical Center (1985–1992) and Kaiser Permanente (1992–2015). She is the co-author with Eric Maisel of Creative Recovery: A Complete Addiction Treatment Program That Uses Your Natural Creativity. *She is on the Editorial Board of* Medical Problems of Performing Artists, *the journal of the Performing Arts Medical Association. Susan explained:*

Psychotherapy groups vary depending upon the type of group. At its best, ongoing group psychotherapy provides the healthy family experience you wished you'd had growing up in the first place. Patterns of interpersonal dynamics—both positive and negative—are explored and become clearer, so change becomes possible.

Group members learn to identify, understand, and express their feelings and allow others to do the same. Connection, validation, and authenticity become one's lived experience rather than distant concepts. From this new vantage point, group members are equipped to forge improved relationships in their real lives outside of therapy.

I've lead different types of groups over the years: time limited cognitive behavioral therapy (CBT) for eating disorders as part of research studies, CBT and dialectical behavior therapy (DBT) for chemical dependency recovery, and ongoing psychodynamic "process" groups for addiction and codependency recovery. Therapy groups can serve various functions—from time-limited skill building around specific problems (e.g. anxiety, depression, emotion regulation, distress tolerance, or relapse prevention) to promoting ongoing interpersonal growth through a focus on the "here and now."

Whatever the type, effective groups have shared purposes and commonalities in which the personal becomes the universal. Generally, people are referred to group therapy by their individual therapist who has seen that broadening the work is timely regarding interpersonal patterns and relationship skills and/or when the person feels significantly isolated in their lives. We might also ask, "Who is *not* a good group therapy candidate?" If a person is in crisis, if they have impulse control problems that threaten others, if they are not willing to honor the group norms/boundaries, and if their character defenses compromise their capacity for empathy and interpersonal relatedness, they are not a good fit for group therapy.

For someone looking for a group to join, the American Group Psychotherapy Association is an excellent resource (see www.agpa.org). Additionally, local therapists often list their groups through their state or county professional associations. If I had a loved one in emotional or mental distress, first I would encourage them to get connected with trustworthy people in their lives. Connection comes in many forms and what a person needs changes over time. At some point, it might well include group psychotherapy work.

Sometimes just starting to find the trust and humility to recognize our vulnerability and talk about that with close friends is enough to feel better. When that is not enough, or when the emotional distress runs deep and involves destructive patterns from early learning, I would encourage my loved one to find an experienced therapist who has seen many people with similar issues. I would let them know that they are not alone and that help is available.

Social Therapy

Christine LaCerva, M.Ed., is Director of the Social Therapy Group in Manhattan and Brooklyn, where she has a highly diverse, group-based practice with clients of all ages. With Fred Newman, the late founder of social therapy, LaCerva has worked for over 34 years to advance a philosophically inspired, postmodern, performatory approach to emotional development, helping clients build environments (everywhere) for emotional growth. Christine explained:

Social therapy is a postmodern group therapy that has at its centerpiece emotional growth and development. Essential to its practice is the philosophical exploration of how human beings have the unique characteristic of being able to simultaneously be who we are and be who we are becoming.

As a social therapist, I am practicing a search for method. This activity is asking philosophical questions that provoke the group to create new kinds of dialogues that go beyond the status quo. Therapists and patients in social therapy groups work together to develop their capacities to live life creatively and investigate the conceptual frameworks that inform how we think and how we have come to feel the way we do.

I have been working with young people diagnosed on the autism spectrum for over 30 years. I have created multi-family groups as a new modality to enhance social communication and foster creative expression for all the family members involved.

The group has patients who have been diagnosed with a variety of labels. Some have no label at all. Mixing the group with young people that are on the spectrum, off the spectrum, have learning problems, or are just generally having a hard time is critical to its success. The families come together, examine the assumptions and biases they bring into their lives, and create a space that challenges the often-ironclad identities of a diagnosis.

In these groups, families get the support they need to loosen their grip on the fears and anxieties about whether their children or teens will be able to fit into a biased society. What they discover through improvisation and performance exercises is that young people on the spectrum (and those who aren't) can create new ways of being, new ways of seeing and feeling in working with others.

Most importantly, parents and young people alike have the opportunity to become powerful in how they are living their lives. They discover their creative potential and intellectual capacities to go beyond themselves. I lead performance games where young people get to play the therapist. Being related to as someone who needs assistance, young people on the spectrum welcome the opportunity to give their thoughts on what would be helpful to others. Their strengths shine through, their labels become less important. Being powerful in life for parents and their kids becomes central.

As a practitioner of social therapy, I do not diagnose the adults and children that come to see me. However, they often arrive with existing labels from prior therapeutic work or, in the case of children, required school assessments. In many cases there are initial conversations about the diagnosis. Some patients feel that it has been helpful to them. Others often say it is merely used to get reimbursement for sessions. Some want to get off their meds but feel they cannot.

The conversations I have about diagnoses have more to do with what we as the patient and therapist want to do with it, if anything. I am only interested in it as far as it has had an impact on the client. I do not see it as an accurate or preferable description of who someone is.

As for psychiatric medications, I think in general mental health professionals can move too quickly to prescribe. I prefer to create new kinds of conversations that deconstruct and creatively reconstruct a variety of activities in group therapy and outside of it that can support the person's ongoing development.

Family Therapy

Marilyn Wedge, Ph.D., is a family therapist with 27 years of experience. She is the author of three books, most recently A Disease Called Childhood: Why ADHD Became an American Epidemic (March, 2016). Dr. Wedge holds a doctorate from the University of Chicago and was a post-doctoral fellow at the Hastings Center for Bioethics. Marilyn explained:

We all live in the context of complex social systems like family, culture, and society. All of these systems influence our behavior and emotions. However, thinking in terms of systems is difficult because systems are non-linear. In other words, a cause in one part of the system may have an effect in another area that does not resemble the cause.

For example, parents have been quarreling and their four-year-old son holds a knife to his throat and threatens to kill himself. The connection between the two events is not obvious. The family therapist seeks out the situation that is affecting the child and causing him to have problems. Instead of asking ourselves "What is wrong with this child?" we ask "What are the stressors in the child's world to which he is reacting?"

This is not the common-sense worldview. In fact, it is counter-intuitive because contemporary thinking is based on a biological frame of internal causes. This is why labeling individuals with mental disorders does not make sense from a family therapy point of view because the actual problem lies in interpersonal relationships.

Even the therapist is part of the system. If a therapist focuses only on "symptoms of a disorder," as the DSM directs, she is going to find them. Then the only solution is to medicate the symptoms, which only hides the true cause of the problem. In contrast, the family therapist examines the child's social context, revealing the stressors to which the child is reacting. Family therapy is particularly effective for children's problems since the family is dominant in the child's social environment.

Peer Mentoring and Counseling

Sande Roberts is the author of We Need to Talk About Suicide. *Roberts has been in the crisis and behavioral health field for over 25 years. She has a master's degree in psychology and is a certified trainer of trainers in suicide prevention and crisis intervention by the State of California Department of Mental Health. As a board member of the Arizona Association for Conflict Resolution, she continues to help schools implement peer-led programs. Sande explained:*

I've worked with teens in various settings since 1990. Programs that work are ones where the youth themselves are mentored and taught skills to help themselves and their friends.

The teen years are challenging and confusing. Youth are experiencing dramatic changes in their bodies, relationships, limits, and values. Peer pressure, rebellion, and curiosity frequently guide decisions. This is a time when people are wondering if the next suicidal, homicidal, or physically or emotionally bullied teen they hear about in the news will be someone they know: someone who lives next door, sits across the aisle at school, or is related to them.

Peer-led teen programs have been around for a long time. Teens talk to, listen to, and believe other teens long before they consult with an adult. Schools with peer helper and conflict resolution programs have teens who are trained in peer education, leadership, listening, and helping skills. The focus is identification and early intervention.

My personal experience has been that teens become enabled to help themselves and their peers cope with a mega-list of relevant issues, including but not limited to: suicide, violence on campus and in the community, intergenerational conflicts, relationship breakups, dangerous relationships, scholastic pressure, teen sexuality, loneliness, real or imagined guilt and/or shame, revenge, drug and alcohol abuse, cultural tension, and low self-esteem.

For parents, it's natural to want to solve problems for their children as well as for close friends and family members. Parents may become frightened by the expression of their children's more intense emotions and respond with strong disbelief or anger, and try to deflect their concerns with statements that cut off communication rather than helping.

In addition to peer helper programs, teens can be helped by being connected with responsible adults including those in big brother/big sister types of mentoring programs. Parenting is challenging under the best of circumstances even if parents aren't dealing with their own broad spectrum of critical issues. Parents of teens and young adults are often generationally sandwiched between the child and their own parents.

Transformational Coaching

Dr. Rosie Kuhn is an international speaker, trainer, and transformational coach in the US, Moscow, London, Prague, and Tel Aviv. All of her work, including her books and blogs, focus on self-empowerment, in service to the fulfillment of the human spirit. Her latest book is Cultivating Spirituality in Children: 101 Ways to Make Every Child's Spirit Soar. *You can find more information about Dr. Rosie Kuhn and her work at www.theparadigmshifts.com. Rosie explained:*

In many ways, coaching and therapy are the same. The biggest difference is that coaching requires the client to take action—practicing new thinking and actions, in alignment with their desired outcome. Therapy does not insist on the client taking action in alignment with any insights they experience through a therapy session.

Both therapy and coaching work toward self-realization and self-actualization. Both work to empower clients to know themselves and to act in alignment with their values, principles, and truths; in essence, to trust and respect themselves. Both therapist and coach are thinking partners for their clients. They support and empower them to live in their highest capacity to thrive.

Therapy works to shift dysfunctional thinking and behavior to functional. It works within the rules of consensus reality. Therapy supports individuals to be "normal." It strengthens an individual's ability to function more effectively within relationships. It provides support and a place to be seen and heard. Therapy cultivates emotional intelligence. The greater the client's emotional intelligence, the more likely they are to be present with their emotions in a respectful way that gives them room to be expressed authentically without the client interfering, restricting, or controlling them. This is the beginning of self-realization and self-actualization.

Coaching is a specific set of skills and tools, with the specific objective of getting clients to their desired end results. It is action based, in that clients have to self-empower themselves to take specific responsibility and accountable actions in the directions they say they want to go. When obstacles present themselves and stop the client from gaining forward momentum, the coach acts as a thinking partner, assisting the client, only through inquiry, to unconceal specific belief patterns.

The tool of inquiry is foundational to coaching, as it reflects the coach's confidence in clients having the ability to source within themselves for what is required to fulfill their desired outcome. In coaching, the client is 100% responsible for the outcome of their interpretations and their actions. The client's total belief system is up for exploration. The client is required to experiment with shifting their beliefs and their actions, only in service to what it is they want.

Coaching stretches and expands the individual's bandwidth of comfort and "what is normal" to include more of their unlimited potential. Coaching takes the client from impossible to possible, by reworking the context of limiting beliefs. At some point, each of us will have to take a leap of faith, again, making the impossible possible. It is the willingness to shift a thought, or an action, for one brief moment of time, time and again. It's training oneself and empowering oneself to take control of all of one's thoughts and actions. Each of us has the capacity to do this work.

Before I became a coach, I was trained as a marriage, family, and child therapist, with an emphasis on systems theory. I believe this training set the groundwork for my coaching practice, as did my training as a spiritual director. From this perspective, every individual is whole and complete, and 100% potentiality. It is only their limiting beliefs and interpretations, which can be unconscious and deeply embedded, that are what restricts them living an optimum life, whatever that means individually.

As a coach, I see people as not having *problems*, but rather *facing human dilemmas*, which pit their higher self and values against that aspect of self that fears annihilation (the ego-self). The question that a coach will ask their clients, no matter what the client is facing is: "What do you want?" Until a person is clear about what it is they want, they won't be able to choose, for themselves, what actions are in alignment with the end result they are wanting. Aside from circumstances that present challenging situations for an individual, problems are caused, more often than not, by a lack of clarity about what is the desired outcome.

The clearer the intended result, the clearer the actions that need to be taken, and the clearer the client becomes about their resistance to following through towards the desired end results.

School Counseling

Chene Walz is a licensed professional counselor in the state of Georgia and holds national credentials as a certified clinical mental health counselor and approved clinical supervisor. She enjoys her work with students at the Savannah College of Art and Design (SCAD), and her areas of clinical interest include trauma, working with artists, GLBT concerns, clinical supervision, and energy psychology interventions. Chene explained:

SCAD strives to lead the way in creating the best art and design education, in part via employing talented faculty and providing advanced learning resources, and also by living a mission that is truly student-centered. This mission includes support services such as those offered through my office. I have been a therapist in the SCAD counseling center since 2001, and I am hard pressed to imagine a better "job" than supporting talented creators in their academic and life endeavors within an institution that values the creative process and cares about both academic and personal success.

Creators as a group seem to have a more deeply felt experience (and freer expression) of emotions as well. Taking these broad ideas into consideration, it's not a far leap to predict what the potential mental and emotional (and physical) manifestations of disruption in this meaning-making process might look like: some configuration of signs and symptoms can include overwhelm, crises of meaning, anxiety, depression, mania, and problems with substance use.

I do believe we see a higher incidence of students with "diagnosable mental disorders" as well as those on the autism spectrum as compared to students at a typical liberal arts college or university. Many students I see for counseling reference their creative work/process as having some direct connection with their presenting concern(s). For instance, a client whose primary issue was trichotillomania (compulsive hair-pulling) was best served to some degree through addressing the intense perfectionism that was causing her to nearly miss deadlines and fulfill her sense of dread that she would not be able to give physical form to what was in her mind.

Most often when we are able to get to the root of the issue and identify corresponding strategies for accepting and transcending it, the flow of the creative process (along with a meaning-full relationship with the work) returns, and often symptoms (including those that amount to a psychiatric diagnosis) significantly remit or disappear completely. Common culprits disrupting the creative process and contributing to mental health concerns are fear, anxiety, and perfectionism all tangled up in various areas of creative life, including: experience of meaning, artist identity, knowledge about navigating the career landscape, procrastination (often because the work can never be good enough and can never be truly "done"), fear of failure, fear of success, fear of mistakes … the list is limitless.

We offer quite a range of comprehensive support services, including creativity coaching as a standalone service. Students experiencing creative paralysis or a loss of meaning in work can find effective interventions here. I facilitate a group that employs energy psychology techniques focused on an approach called acutapping (or emotional freedom techniques/EFT) which can be easily taught and applied to most any issue that is correlated with emotional (or physical) intensity, and I also use this intervention in individual therapy to treat many concerns, especially anxiety and trauma.

***

The goal of this chapter is to remind practitioners that the practice of diagnosing and prescribing is not the only option available to parents looking for help for their distressed, disturbed, or difficult child. Helpers already know this but they tend to forget this truth, given the ubiquity of the diagnose-and-prescribe model and even if they themselves are working in some alternative way. I hope this chapter proves a useful reminder that the landscape of helping is not limited to the dominant diagnose-and-prescribe paradigm.

8

ORGANIZATIONAL RESOURCES

If your client is dealing with a child in distress, she's likely to be sent or led, perhaps by a school counselor, perhaps by her child's pediatrician, or perhaps by something she's heard, read, or been told, to a child psychologist, child psychiatrist, child psychotherapist, or family therapist.

She's rather less likely to learn about or make use of the other sorts of resources that are available to her. In this chapter I want to introduce you to a number of organizations, so as to give you a sense of what sorts of alternative help may be available to your parent-clients. This is nothing like a comprehensive picture but it will alert you to the sorts of resources that are available.

It's About Childhood & Family, Inc.

Michael Gilbert, Psy.D., has worked in human services for more than 25 years, including foster care, group home, and hospital settings. In addition, he has worked for the past 19 years as a school psychologist within Syracuse City Schools as well as an adjunct professor at local colleges. In 2000, he founded It's About Childhood & Family, Inc. (IACAF), a not-for-profit resource center, as a grassroots movement to provide families with an alternative to the traditional mental health system. Dr. Gilbert is on the board of directors for the International Society of Ethical Psychiatry and Psychology (ISEPP) as well as the annual conference chairperson. Dr. Gilbert received the Friend of Children Award in 2011 and the New York State Psychologist of the Year Award in 2014. He explained:

Our mission at "It's About Childhood & Family Inc." is to empower families to develop independence in handling life's struggles. We utilize a collaborative and trauma informed framework that is not reliant upon a label or diagnosis. Instead we focus on strengths, resources, resiliencies, and potential for growth.

We strive to more accurately inform parents, schools, and the larger community about issues related to mental health: for example, misuse of diagnostic labels, lack of efficacy with prescription drugs, and factors that contribute to social-emotional distress. IACAF uses a "pay-it-forward" approach and families can "pay" for services by volunteering within their community. We provide individual and group counseling and skill building supports.

Throughout the year we offer workshops and trainings for professionals and parents. In addition, we organize one or two conferences per year on a variety of topics such as trauma-informed care, concerns with labels and psychotropic drugs, and approaches to improve the social/emotional/behavioral wellbeing of children. We have brought in national and international experts in the field. Our goal is to provide a more accurate perspective and to have a dialogue about why and how to change the current mental health system, particularly for children.

We believe that families should ultimately be in charge of the care they receive and that youth need to have choices in the types of support they are willing to explore. Therefore, we encourage and provide access to a variety of approaches—such as mindfulness (e.g. meditation, yoga), physical activity (e.g. running, martial arts, boxing), expressive arts (e.g. painting, pottery, photography, writing, music, dance), and relationship building (e.g. nurtured heart approach, peace circles, service learning, mentoring, volunteering).

In addition, we ask families to rule out potential factors that might be contributing to the concerns. This would include examining sleep patterns, nutrition, exercise, computer and television screen time, potential traumatic events, family dynamics, peer groups, educational demands, and other factors.

If the gauge of the health of a society is how well it cares for its youngest members, we are clearly failing. Our youth have become, in large part, collateral damage. Our current systems are not set up in the best interest of our children. They are about special interest, greed, power, and politics. This includes our educational system, which continues to be a significant contributor to children being labeled as "mentally ill" and prescribed a variety of psychotropic medications.

If I had loved ones in emotional distress, I would try and surround them with as much support and nurturance as they were willing to accept. Additionally, I would want them to make an informed decision and would offer resources for them to explore. I would suggest a variety of possible activities that they could consider giving a try—talking with someone (individually or in a group), mindfulness, exercise (walking, running, biking, etc.), gardening, expressive arts, and so on.

I believe they should incorporate their entire body and senses as they process the distress they are going through. I would encourage them to try and connect with things they are passionate about (e.g. cooking, painting, music) and to spend time in those activities. However, I would want them to understand that they have my unconditional support even if they choose to pursue an option, such as medication, that I might not be in agreement with. My hope would be that if medication was tried it would be for the short term and that they explore other approaches simultaneously.

Families Healing Together

Krista Mackinnon has worked with families in mental health recovery for over 10 years. She is a mom to three boys, a yoga teacher and student, and the founding director of Families Healing Together. She believes deeply in the power of hope and possibility. Krista explained:

I was diagnosed in my formative years, at 16, with bipolar disorder, but I didn't believe that "story," or label, or the so-called drugs prescribed to treat it. In my heart, I identified as an artist, a mystic, and a creative. I was told I'd have to spend the rest of my life on medication and that I could anticipate it would still be a struggle to participate in the basics of society. When I learned that there were no blood tests, X-rays, or hard evidence to prove that I had this illness/disability I decided not to believe in it.

I felt insulted by what I considered to be their "fortune telling" of my future, and I had a deep-seated knowing that they actually had no idea who I was, or what I was capable of becoming. They were predicting that I'd have a difficult life filled with struggle and sadness, and that my disability would hold me back. Instead of believing them, I began crafting a preferred future for myself based on the alternative belief that I was an incredibly unique yet misunderstood person with important gifts to contribute to the world.

Families Healing Together helps families to understand and cope with the complicated experience of extreme distress, psychosis, and psychiatric labeling. Traditionally, when someone in a family is given a psychiatric diagnosis, families are educated to understand the experience from a brain disease/medical perspective, and often aren't given much else in terms of tools on how to heal and move forward as a family.

The philosophy of Families Healing Together is to consider all information with a critical perspective. Instead of focusing on causes, symptoms, and explanations, we propose to instead focus on deeply connected interpersonal relating, healing, and hope. We do this by sharing a curriculum filled with powerful recovery stories, helpful communication tools, and informative theories and articles about human nature. People in the class give and get support from one another as they share their personal responses to the content, and they find solace in knowing they aren't alone in the journey.

People in the class discuss everything from orthomolecular treatment to electroconvulsive therapy, but Families Healing Together offers no medical advice. It takes a relational approach to mostly everything, including medications. The question of medications can be complex in families with intense dynamics and hidden meanings, old hurts, and trust triggers. We encourage families to dissect power dynamics, to weigh the pros and cons of psychiatric treatment from a "quality of life" perspective, to explore their biggest fears and hopes together, and to create crisis/wellness plans together.

In most families where disagreements around treatment arise, the problems are usually founded on secrecy, hiding, fear, and lack of connection. Some people are taking their prescribed medications, some are trying to come off medications, and some are painfully over-medicated; but these circumstances are not what Families Healing Together places specific attention on. The goal from a family recovery perspective is to focus on strengthening the connection and communication around the circumstances.

We also offer online courses. Online classes are great for a number of reasons:

1. As long as you have an internet connection, the support is open and available to you at all hours.
2. You can be completely anonymous if you choose to be, which can be incredibly liberating for many people.
3. You don't have to reorganize your life to "attend" class because you engage with the materials as needed, at your own convenience.
4. If you are struggling emotionally, communicating in person can sometimes feel like a challenging barrier. Communicating complex emotional concepts and epiphanies in bed in your pajamas at two a.m. in the moment you feel inspired and compelled to reach out is a real gift.
5. It is unifying. People from all over the world take the class, so inevitably there is great diversity in the class, which translates to very rich and multi-faceted discussions.

If I had a loved one in emotional or mental distress, I would suggest the following. Try to avoid power struggles and/or getting locked into patterns of non-communication. The best way to do this is to let your heart be vulnerable and open to the person you love as much as possible. Be as curious as you can be about their experience and reality in the moment while simultaneously suspending your judgments, interpretations, and advice. Align yourself with them as an ally by valiantly focusing on their strengths, power, possibility, and potential.

Believe in them completely while staying unattached to outcomes and having faith in your own patience. In the process, pay close attention to your inner landscape so that you don't get compassion fatigue and subconsciously become resentful. If you start noticing internal tiredness or frustration take action right away by ramping up your self-care practices and setting any boundaries or limits that need to be communicated.

Most importantly, remind yourself daily that the only person you have control over is your own self, and focus much of your energy and effort on being your best self, because that will ripple positively towards everyone you love in beautiful ways you can't even imagine.

Artreach, Inc.

Rebecca Atkins is a licensed professional counselor, creativity coach, and Executive Director of Artreach, Inc. She enjoys singing, songwriting, and playing bass, and has written and performed sketch and stand-up comedy about mental health issues since 1993. Becca is passionate about helping humans connect with themselves and with others through the arts. Becca explained:

I work at Artreach, Inc., a non-profit mental health and arts agency based in Norwich, Connecticut. Our vision is of a world where a psychiatric diagnosis is not a limiting factor for participating in life. We bring meaning and joy to people's lives through creativity and human connection.

Artreach started in 1985 as The Second Step Players, a mental health sketch comedy theater troupe. In 2010, we expanded to include Comic Alchemy, a stand-up comedy team trained by David Granirer, founder of Stand Up For Mental Health. The actors, who have psychiatric diagnoses, write and perform comedy designed to change negative perceptions about people who have mental illnesses.

Artreach also offers a walking club; a music program and jazz group; and classes in playwriting, poetry, and visual arts taught by local artists. We operate as a community of practice. The group creates their experience together, with a focus on creativity, fun and non-judgment of self and others.

When we first meet a new member, we describe Artreach's culture as an oasis where people can take a break from their symptoms. This suggestion, coupled with the supportive environment and positive role modeling of seasoned members, creates an opening for the creation of an oasis to happen.

We ask everyone to leave their diagnosis at the door and simply participate in the rehearsal or class. Daily drama is also left at the door, so people can practice stepping outside of their repetitive story. Kindness and treating each other with respect help establish the container for creating. In this environment, people feel supported to expand and try new things.

We're not asking people to pretend to be happy when they're not, but to notice how they feel, and to participate as they can on that day. Most often, something will shift for the better by the end of the rehearsal or class. This is a hopeful reminder that it's worth it to engage even when you don't feel great. It's powerful to recognize that participating in something you care about changes feelings and can change them again.

The arts are particularly healing for someone in mental distress. The arts are great for building self-esteem, practicing teamwork, allowing for self-expression, and more. Having something to work on that matters to you provides structure to your day and gives a sense of meaning. At Artreach, we focus on using the arts to heal on three levels: personally, interpersonally, and in the community, by shifting perspectives through performances.

There are additional benefits to performing theater and music. Humans want to belong. When people experience psychiatric symptoms, they may sense themselves as flawed, as "other." Working on a common goal like a performance, everyone has a stake in bringing the project to life. Each person shares responsibility for the end result and can see the value of their participation.

Another benefit of performing is learning to feel fear, yet not letting it stop you. One way to do this is to recognize and make use of the support that is available.

Many people are surrounded by support but are unaccustomed to noticing that. Practicing recognizing and making use of the support, whether internally or from another person, is a skill that can be generalized to everyday life. I see the current "mental disorder" paradigm as a complex paradigm that has serious limitations. If you view a diagnosis as something real and concrete, you have an incomplete picture. We humans are a complex lot, and no description of a set of symptoms can encapsulate everything that drives emotional distress.

Recovery from mental distress can and does happen, given the right supports for the situation. It takes work, though, and can be hard. I don't believe medication alone is enough, and it can sometimes make things worse. I feel each person should find whatever helps, and do that. There are ways to learn coping skills to manage or eliminate distressing symptoms. It's a matter of finding the right kind of therapy, support group, nutrition, exercise regimen, and/or medication. What works is unique to each individual.

If I had a loved one in emotional or mental distress, I would first look at current life circumstances. Causes like physical illness, poor nutrition, and poverty often get overlooked. Any of these can create distress, and can be difficult to change without intervention. A good therapist or other professional skilled in treating the type of symptoms they are experiencing can help. The right fit is unique to each person and situation. Other things to try are mindfulness meditation and support groups.

I'd like to mention something less common that helped me personally with depression and anxiety. My symptoms changed dramatically after I took a full impact self-defense course. It enabled me to embody a sense of safety and personal power in a visceral way. Working outside of class with a therapist helped metabolize the experience.

I would be remiss if I didn't add that a daily creative practice can be wonderfully healing. In the arts world, there are options for solitary learning and practice, for connecting with others in a community of practice, and for sharing your work through performances or art shows. I've seen theater, music, and writing reduce mental distress and improve people's lives in some amazing ways.

Creating Communities

Rob Levit is a multi-award winning creative artist and musician, non-profit director, and speaker on creativity living in Annapolis, Maryland. He is a 2013 Innovator of the Year recipient from the Maryland Daily Record and 2011 Martin Luther King Peace Maker Award recipient for his work with youth and adults using the arts as a path to build life skills. Rob explained:

I'm the founder of Creating Communities, an organization that mentors at-risk youth and adults by teaching "life skills through the arts." Many years ago, I was performing at a Title I elementary school, in other words, a school in a low-income area. One of the activities I did during the school-wide assembly was bring students up to scat sing the blues with my jazz trio. On that particular morning, an eager boy was waving his hands in the front row to come up and so I called him. Behind him were his teachers and they were sort of waving me off as if to say "Don't bring that kid up there!" Alas, it was too late.

As the music kicked in, with my assistance, the boy began to scat sing beautifully and soulfully! The audience cheered and his teachers were in shock. After the assembly, the principal rushed up to me and said "That child has a terrible stutter and his teachers were worried he would fail." At that moment, I had an epiphany—how many opportunities for personal growth do children and adults miss because their teachers and mentors don't have the skill set or creative imagination to see possibilities and potential in those they work with?

Unfortunately, it is far too many. Don't get me wrong—these were excellent teachers—but they were conditioned by their own perceptions, fears, and challenges, as we all are. After I left the school, I began to have a nagging feeling, or better yet a prompting. I wondered how many lives could be positively impacted if we stopped teaching kids and adults and instead collaborated and partnered with them to reveal their otherwise hidden and untapped gifts? That was really the genesis of Creating Communities. It would be many years later that I finally had the creative courage to put a structure and plan around my desire to make a difference through the arts.

Almost 10 years later, we have worked with hundreds and hundreds of kids and adults, connecting them with their own innate abilities. So much of education is learning to see past our own inability to understand the latent potential in people and, frankly, in ourselves. Think about what all successful creative people need to do: design, collaborate, communicate intent, persist, visualize, and overcome blocks for starters. Each of our Creating Communities programs gently offers participants the opportunities to discover and engage in their own creative work.

For example, during our summer Arts Mentorship Academy, 60 youth of all ages gather for five days of intensive dance, visual art, creative writing, world drumming and singing, along with mentoring and cultural enrichment activities. Here they are challenged to sit with kids they wouldn't normally choose to sit with, clean up messes they didn't make, and, in just a week, start and finish several projects that a couple of hundred family and community members will watch on closing day.

In my mind, and as I've learned, those are some good life skills to acquire! There is usually so much emphasis on individual achievement but when you are truly "creating communities" the life skills acquired are about trusting each other, depending on each other, and pushing each other in ways that we didn't know we were capable of. In many ways, it's an uncommon message in our current "there's an app for that" world. We ask our kids to look past likes and dislikes and find the meaning on the other side of their limits.

In these ways art teaches life skills. When our mouths sing beautiful melodies, when our hands create new paintings and sculptures, when we move with each other in sync to a cool rhythm, our entire sensory system becomes engaged in learning—and that's learning through direct experience. Too often, we start with "book learning" and "butts in seats." That's all well and good, and at the same time it's great to just dive headlong into experiences not knowing what the results will look like.

We want students to recognize great work as it emerges from them. There's not necessarily a template to follow to get there. To me, that's more life-like than a cerebral study of the arts. I mean, how many lectures on teamwork and collaboration can kids hear?

When we get them playing African drums and singing within a half hour of meeting each other, the life lessons become self-evident. You can see the look on the face of a child who in rehearsal jumps higher than ever before, sings a solo in front of the group, or reads a heart-felt poem in front of strangers. It's priceless.

So, a major part of the Creating Communities Way is through embodied and multi-sensory learning; thinking is awesome, but at some point, you have to do stuff to move your life along. The kids take positive risks and we are there to support them. Here are a few anecdotes to paint a fuller picture:

- One summer, we had an autistic youth at the Arts Mentorship Academy. At the end of the week one of our mentors told me that the youth's guardians approached her at the final reception and asked, "What did you all do to our child?" She asked, "What do you

mean?" They answered, "He's actually talking to us!" They were absolutely delighted and had no idea that their own child could sing, dance, and speak on stage.
- One of my students has been with Creating Communities since middle school and she's now in her early twenties. She's seen some hard times in life, harder than most of us will ever understand, and she still attends virtually all of our programs and serves as a support staff and mentor to the young kids. The art and the mentoring provide her with "scaffolding" for her sometimes chaotic family situation. The programs bring her comfort because she can drop all the life baggage, leave it at the door, and get engaged in activities that generate personal meaning.
- When we had our "Life Skills Through the Arts" Program at a drug addiction facility a few years ago, one of the patients was brought in with ankle cuffs and handcuffs. He was in sad shape. I was worried about reaching him in the group session. At the time, I was teaching "Rob-chi," my very bad yet simple version of meditative movement. I just wanted the patients to be in their bodies again and appreciate the joy of movement and connection and so they changed the practice from "Rob-chi" to, for example, "Bill-chi" or "Sue-chi." Later I was told by one of the main staff members that the young man who had been brought in via hand and ankle cuffs was spotted doing his own "chi" in the mornings before anyone was around. That feeling of being there, assisting someone to wake up to their own innate self-healing and self-learning potential, that's what it's all about.

There are some cardinal rules to being a great mentor. The first one is to listen. How many kids are actually listened to? We so badly want to fix or correct a "troubled" or challenging kid without really, really, just being there for them. We have to stop the tendency to want to speak or lecture. And, even before listening actually, we need to create an atmosphere of safety. Why would a kid share their fears and pain with us when they don't feel safe?

We can't be afraid to show emotion, either. It's OK to let kids know that when they hurt, you hurt and when they feel joy, you feel joy. We are taught to be at arm's length from those we serve, but how then does that build trust? Of course, we keep our professional composure and at the same time we need to meet kids at the level that they can feel comfortable sharing. So many kids, especially in the field that I am in, lack consistent adults who care.

I'll close with this: recently a kid I know was thrown out of the classroom at a school I visit. He started to have a meltdown and before I knew it administrators were called as well as the resource officer. Fortunately, they did a great job speaking with the student and he was admitted back into class. Later, I was able to speak with the student, creating safety, listening, and empathizing. The student shared his deep anger over the fighting and conflict between the parents. Finally, when the moment was right, I asked, "What's underneath the anger?" The student said "Sadness." See, kids are smart and they are self-aware! We just have to create the opportunity and facilitate their growth and awareness.

Before we judge them as aggressive, angry, or bad, have we done all we can do to reach them? Or, are we projecting what we think they are onto them? It is imperative to stay open! Have we created opportunities to learn, grow, and succeed in a way that resonates with their natural abilities? I think as educators, we have a long way to go. A large part of it is understanding our own feelings and emotions and not being so quick to shove them aside. Instead of resisting the truth that life is difficult, let's get to know it, understand it, and create within it.

The Extended Therapy Room

Carina Hakansson, Ph.D., is a social worker, psychotherapist, founder of the Family Care Foundation and the Extended Therapy Room Foundation, and the mother of two lovely sons. Carina explained:

The story of the Family Care Foundation is a long one. But, very briefly, it started as a reaction towards a system which far too often seemed to have forgotten important principles about human beings and life conditions. I was angry, but also very determined to try together with others to create a place which should be good to stay at, not just for those called clients, but also for the professional "helpers" and the family homes involved, as well as for the people around the so-called client: family, friends, and others.

We had an idea to try to combine essential knowledge from ordinary life with important knowledge from the professional fields, mainly within therapy and social work. The organization has grown over the years, and has become part of a worldwide network, so much so that a new foundation started last autumn with the aim to extend our experience into a wider context, by research, training, and of course therapeutic practice, which is still the most essential part of the process. "Practice comes first" is a statement we hold in very high regard. The name of the new organization is the Extended Therapy Room Foundation.

I've written about this in a book called *Ordinary Life Therapy*. The book is about practice and theoretical ideas at the Family Care Foundation and describes the collaborative work involving those called clients, their families, family homes, and staff at the office, mainly therapists. It is written in a personal way and includes my own reactions, thoughts, feelings, and visions. There are narratives from different perspectives, interviews with some family homes and clients, some stories from my own life and history, some poems, and some philosophical ideas and wonderings.

We need to find ways to let people know that other narratives different from the current paradigm exist. So, the effort is to create a worldwide proud and skilled network including researchers, practitioners, and people with lived experience, not just in the fields of psychotherapy and psychiatry but far beyond that. Artists, farmers, economists, students, statisticians, carpenters, dancers ... you name it, people of all kind, since this is an issue which has to do with each and every one of us.

I am very worried about the current situation and I am sad and upset by the way children and young people are defined and "treated" by pharmaceuticals. This is a problem for society as a whole. If I had a loved one in emotional or mental distress, I would suggest that he or she not go to a psychiatrist. Let him scream and cry and shout if necessary, but not on the street and not in a psychiatric ward. I would hope that we, the people around him, were enough: that there would be many people to stay around him during the most critical moment and to not let the fear overwhelm either the person whom it concerns or those of us who are nearby.

The Extended Therapy Room Foundation is an alternative to the psychiatric system, and we use no psychiatric diagnosis language when we talk with those called clients or when talking about them. We have many years of experience knowing that there are possibilities to reduce or withdraw psychiatric drugs if something else is "offered," as for example a context where people are trying to make sense of what is happening or has happened in life.

Sometimes it is also necessary to create a physical safe space, so we work closely together with some family homes that are a kind of foster home, where the one called client may stay for a shorter or a longer period of time. Those of us working as therapists are involved and support both the family home and the client. An essential part of our work is to let people know that there are alternatives to the biological model and that we are blessed to be part of a great global network that is inspiring and enriching in so many ways.

The Rogue & Rouge Foundation

Nicole Gibson is committed to making a positive difference in the lives of young people. After overcoming mental health challenges as a young person, in particular anorexia nervosa, she is channeling her energy into motivating other young people to be the best they can be. In 2011, she established The Rogue & Rouge Foundation to reverse the stigmatization of mental health, body image, and self-esteem issues in Australia's young people. She is tackling her social cause through the creation of community outreach programs, working directly with schools, service providers, and education departments in both central and remote parts of Australia. Ms. Gibson was a finalist for Young Australian of the Year 2014, one of Australia's top 100 most influential women, was appointed onto the National Mental Health Commission as the youngest ever commissioner, and won the Pride of Australia Inspiration Medal in 2014. Nicole explained:

I founded The Rogue & Rouge Foundation in 2011, on my 18th birthday, after a personal experience with anorexia nervosa alongside other mental health challenges throughout the most formative and impressionable years of my life. The foundation takes an entirely different approach towards mental health, one that's entirely community based and non-clinical. Through engaging young people through schools and community groups, alongside service providers, parents, and teachers to cultivate much needed discussion, we believe that mental health can be tackled as a normal part of everyday life.

After working in 300 communities Australia-wide, and impacting more than a quarter of a million young Australians, the team is truly convinced that the largest national contributor to mental ill health is disconnection. By creating a generation of young Australians that understand how to authentically connect to themselves, each other, and their passion in life, by learning to become their own masters, we can create a population of Australians that lead fulfilled, healthy, and inspiring lives.

Our programs were written after a team of four of us traveled Australia in vans as teenagers, conducting Australia's largest hands-on research into youth mental health. We now deliver our programs through schools, universities, community groups, and work places. I believe all stress, regardless of age, comes down to the same root cause: a lack of alignment with self and purpose. I believe in today's world we are often stifled and bombarded with thousands of opinions on what to do, who to be, what to think, what to conform to; and that we lose our own voice.

We can no longer hear the voice inside of us, guiding us in the right direction. Anxiety and stress often come down to this misalignment, and in order to shift this, time in stillness is crucial, time away from the loudness of the world, to connect within. Every person will find this in a different way; whether that be meditation, mindfulness practice, running (sports), or otherwise.

It's important for schools to remember that they can't be everything for their students. But they can make use of the valuable community organizations that exist and that specialize in the delivery of education and information; and from my point of view it's the school's role to take initiative and form crucial relationships with these external organizations.

The relationship an objective facilitator can form with a student, in my experience, is a necessary consideration when it comes to this work. Young people will often tell me it's far easier to open up to someone who's a little bit removed from their everyday world, who's closer in age, and more easily relatable. For schools, it's essential to create on-going opportunities for young people to engage with this work at different ages and different intellectual and emotional levels.

As to psychiatric medication, I like to take a bit of a different view to most. I honestly feel that our responsibility here on Earth is to learn to master ourselves, and what happens in another's journey is not up to us to judge or formulate opinions. Personally, I feel it's important to understand our minds and bodies free of any substances; however, that's based on my own disciplines and practice, and I try and steer clear of dictating or voicing my options to others.

The most important thing to create for anyone, in particular a loved one, is a space of total permission and acceptance. It's only through complete acceptance that a person can understand and process exactly what's present for them. It is not our responsibility to advise or give answers to someone else; we are the most qualified to make our own decisions. I feel that the best thing we can do for others is allow them to be exactly as they are, and this provides a platform of genuine healing.

The best way to create this for another person is to step away from your ego, to let go of the need to "fix" or "save" someone, and realize that by playing the hero, that automatically puts the other person in the role of victim. No one is a victim of their circumstances; they in fact contribute to creating them. It requires a strong degree of empowerment to move through challenge, adversity, trauma, and distress, and this can only be accessed when the individual is empowered to take responsibility for themselves and their choices.

***

These six examples can't possibly tell the full story. But hopefully they are eye-opening and suggestive.

What's going on in your own community? Which organizations with a world-wide reach might you like to learn more about? Naturally, you can't be expected to become an expert on all such organizations or to compile a comprehensive dossier on them. But you could learn about a few of them, so as to educate yourself about the alternatives available to your parent-clients. At the very least, you can alert your parent-clients to the fact that more is available to them than what psychiatry or psychotherapy can offer; and you can send them off on their own, possibly invaluable, investigations.

9

ALTERNATIVES FOR "SERIOUS MENTAL ILLNESS"

Some percentage of your parent-clients will be dealing with a child with severe difficulties of the sort traditionally referred to as "serious mental illness." While they may make up only a relatively small percentage of your parent-clients, they will be dealing with an issue so pressing and so enormous that any help (and hope) you can offer them will prove invaluable and a blessing.

In this chapter, I want to provide you with several alternate visions to the current diagnose-and-treat-with-chemicals paradigm and alert you to resources about which you may not be aware. Getting acquainted with these alternate visions and available resources will make you a more educated helper and will aid you in your conversations with your parent-clients who are dealing with a seriously troubled or troubling child.

Gould Farm

Jane Linsley has been working in the field of mental health and addictions for over 30 years and on the Gould Farm Clinical Team since 2004. She has been Clinical Director of the team since 2006. A graduate of Smith School for Social Work, she is licensed in social work and addictions, with additional certifications in both trauma and women's relational theory of mental health. She has as an ongoing passion for beneficial new therapies and work in the area of mental health care, as well as an ongoing, and long-standing, passion for how people relate to issues of inclusion and the shame resulting from stigma—both for the individual and as a culture.

Eric Maisel: Can you tell us a little bit about Gould Farm?

Jane Linsley: Gould Farm is a therapeutic community for people living with mental health challenges. Our residential treatment program is located on a 700-acre farm in western Massachusetts. Residents (who are referred to as "guests") join in the work of the farm and community, tending to animals, growing vegetables, baking bread, making meals, and even helping run a small cafe. When guests are ready to move on, we have a continuum of care including transition homes in Boston and the Berkshires and an extended community that supports lifelong recovery.

EM: Would you say that you have an underlying philosophy with regard to what helps people in distress?

JL: The broad strokes of recovery at Gould Farm encompass purposeful work and service, and relationship with self and others in a community that fosters recovery and a sense of possibility. The Farm itself enables a sense of connection with place and nature. Our therapeutic model provides the time and space for an individual to include their own experience and voice in creating a narrative of what has happened that brings them to this moment in time. Through these beliefs, our staff and guests collaborate to explore strengths and abilities to reengage with a life of meaning beyond a diagnosis or crisis.

EM: What are your thoughts about so-called psychiatric medication as it relates to the folks you serve?

JL: For some, medication is an important tool and for others it is not. Our psychiatrist is a part of a network of support that surrounds each guest. That network (staff, peers, and family) provides a continuum of care for the entire time they are with us and can give active feedback and support about the use of medication or other supports for stability.

If medication is necessary we hope always to find the lowest dosage of a medication that will enable a person to stabilize a pattern that may have emerged in crisis or in its aftermath. No two people are alike and therefore how medicine fits in a holistic picture of health varies with each person we encounter.

We are fortunate to be a setting where we can support people in making medication adjustments that enable them to form a relationship with a medication. This can be a process. We try to understand the role of medication within a holistic picture of who a person is.

EM: If you had a loved one in emotional or mental distress, what would you suggest that he or she do or try?

JL: I believe in what I do and the model we are. I would want them to have the opportunity to be heard, to include their experience and understanding in the narrative of what is happening. I would want them to be able to be supported in seeing abilities and strengths in their daily structure, to have connections, and to have a network of support that followed them in their journey. I would want them to have relationships over time with treaters who knew them and who took the time to know me and the rest of the network of support available.

I would want them to have community and meaningful structure in their days and connection and fun in their downtime. I would want healthy food and an understanding of the role of food and nutrition as well as medicine and therapy. I would wholeheartedly want for a loved one to have an experience like Gould Farm as a foundation for the journey of healing that is life.

The Spiritual Crisis Network

Catherine G. Lucas is an author, teacher, and speaker on the subject of mental health and spirituality. She brings conscious activism to her role as Project Coordinator for the new Alliance for Revisioning Mental Health. Catherine is also Founder of the UK Spiritual Crisis Network, a mindfulness trainer, and author of two books, with two more on the way.

Eric Maisel: What is the Spiritual Crisis Network?

Catherine Lucas: The Spiritual Crisis Network (SCN) is a UK charity that comes directly out of personal experience of psychospiritual crisis, both mine and others who were involved in setting it up in 2004. The year before I had been through a brief crisis that was so intense I ended up in a wheelchair for a few days because my legs gave way.

I felt we needed to raise awareness and understanding about the complex relationship between "madness" and mysticism. The SCN offers information and support, mainly by email, to those going through crisis, as well as to family, friends, and professionals. There is a team of volunteers, some who have personal experience, some professional expertise, and some combine both.

There are many equivalent organizations around the world that have also grown up out of transpersonal psychology, including the Canadian Spiritual Emergence Service, the US Spiritual Emergence Network, and other SENs in countries from Germany to Australia and more.

EM: *You've written a book called* Coping with a Mental Health Crisis: Seven Steps to Healing. *What are some of your top headlines and tips from that book?*

CL: That a mental health crisis can be a wake-up call, our psyche's attempt to heal itself; and that it can be an opportunity for healing and growth, given the right understanding and support. I look at mental health from the perspective of transpersonal psychology, that branch of psychology that brings together present-day psychological theory and research with ancient spiritual wisdom.

Every crisis holds the potential to be deeply transformative. To help others fulfill that potential, I've identified Seven Steps to Healing. From taking responsibility for our healing, to reaching out for support, from finding the right health care professionals, to focusing on success stories, the steps are very practical and doable. At the same time, if we really engage with them, they are radical and life-changing.

When we take an integrative approach to mental health care we can combine the very best of mainstream options with more holistic modalities. I encourage people to create their personal path to well-being by exploring which approaches work for them, from mindfulness and open dialogue to transpersonal psychotherapy, homeopathy, family constellations, and more.

Because I've completely turned my life around I know others can too. The book is my encouragement to find the deeper meaning to our mental health struggles, to think outside the "illness" box. When we're able to drop the "illness" label that's when healing and growth become possible.

EM: You've also written the book In Case of Spiritual Emergency. *What would you like to share about that book?*

CL: *In Case of Spiritual Emergency* was my first book and explores the relationship between breakdown and breakthrough in much more depth. For me, pinning psychiatric labels on a process that is about healing and awakening is not that helpful; it misses the point.

All my work comes directly out of my personal experience and what we've learnt through the SCN. So, with *In Case of Spiritual Emergency* I outline the Three Key Phases of moving successfully through spiritual emergency into emergence:

Phase 1: Coping with the Crisis—getting through the worst of it and staying safe.

Phase 2: Making Sense of It All—using the Hero's Journey to help us integrate all we've been through.

Phase 3: Going Back Out into the World—taking our learning and gifts into our everyday lives, sharing with the wider community, and being of service in some way.

The key tool I recommend for getting through the worst is mindfulness. When I was in crisis and ended up in the wheelchair, I discovered how powerful mindfulness can be in such situations. By then I had been meditating for a number of years and I was able to watch the antics of the mind, to see how fear was impacting on my thinking. A direct consequence of that was deciding to train to become a mindfulness teacher.

EM: What are your thoughts on the current, dominant paradigm of diagnosing and treating mental disorders and the use of so-called psychiatric medication to treat mental disorders in children, teens, and adults?

CL: I personally don't feel comfortable with terms like "mental disorders" or "mental illness." I do my best not to use them. I see our mental health struggles and distress as signs that there is healing work to do, that our psyches and souls need tending to.

It's now crystal clear, thanks to the work of people like Robert Whitaker in the USA and James Davies in the UK, that whilst medication has its place, the only thing it can possibly hope to do is control symptoms, rather than offering any long-term healing. For me, it's about learning to manage sensitivity, not just dealing with symptoms. Fortunately, a lot of us are now moving beyond the current paradigm. The medical model is no longer enough to create the kind of healing our society needs. In the same way that Newtonian physics is no longer enough to explain the laws of the universe and has given way to quantum physics, so the current paradigm is being replaced by a broader, more holistic understanding.

EM: *If you had a loved one in emotional or mental distress, what would you suggest that he or she do or try?*

CL: I'd like to reflect here on my own experience of what has helped me when in distress. I've been through at least three periods of acute crisis in my life, the first of which landed me in hospital, on an acute psychiatric ward, and the other two that resulted in a complete transformation of my entire life. The one thing that made the biggest difference between first ending up in hospital and later being able to reclaim my life was, in the later crises, having people around me supporting me who validated rather than pathologized what I was going through. In other words, people who didn't label me as ill, who were not afraid of what was happening; people who believed in me, who believed in the potential of crisis to be transformative.

The Hearing Voices Network

Jacqui Dillon is a respected speaker, writer, and activist, and has lectured and published worldwide on trauma, psychosis, dissociation, and recovery. Jacqui is the national Chair of the Hearing Voices Network in England, Honorary Lecturer in Clinical Psychology at the University of East London, and Honorary Research Fellow in the School of Medicine, Pharmacy and Health, Durham University. Jacqui is the co-editor of *Living with Voices, Demedicalising Misery: Psychiatry, Psychology and the Human Condition*, and the second edition of *Models of Madness: Psychological, Social and Biological Approaches to Psychosis*. Jacqui is also a voice-hearer.

Eric Maisel: *Can you tell us about the Hearing Voices Network, its intentions and activities?*

Jacqui Dillon: The Hearing Voices Network (HVN) in England is an influential, grassroots organization, which works to promote acceptance and understanding of hearing voices, seeing visions, and other unusual sensory experiences. HVN is a collaboration between experts by experience (voice-hearers and family members) who work in partnership with experts by profession (academics, clinicians, and activists) to question, critique, and reframe traditional biomedical understandings of voice-hearing.

As the limits of a solely medical approach to hearing voices and other unusual perceptions becomes more widely known, and people become better informed about alternatives, there has been a growing acceptance by mainstream mental health providers of the approaches that we promote. Rather than being seen as a radical, fringe activity, HVN in England, which is probably the most well-established and well-developed network in the world, now has more than 180 groups operating in many conventional mental health settings, including child and adolescent mental health services, prisons, inpatient units, secure units as well as in community settings.

The position advocated by HVN—that hearing voices and other unusual sensory perceptions are common human experiences, for which there are many explanations—provides a much-needed antidote to the dominant medical discourse which deems these experiences as symptoms of serious mental illnesses, which need to be suppressed and eradicated with medication. Although some people find these approaches helpful, many do not. Finding a safe, confidential space to share your experiences with other people who are accepting of you and your voices and who are trying to understand the meaning of these experiences in order to make better peace with them, has been a transformative and healing experience for many.

EM: *The Hearing Voices Movement is international in scope. Are there differences and similarities from country to country and culture to culture?*

JD: A testament to the significance and impact of the work of the Hearing Voices Movement is its rapid expansion across the world. Over the past 25 years we have seen the development of 33 national HVNs, spread across Europe, North America, Australia, New Zealand, Latin America, and Africa, with practically no material support of any kind. These developments are coordinated by Intervoice (the international coordinating body for the HVM and allied Hearing Voices Networks).

Although the experience of hearing voices is solitary, complex, and varies from person to person, and some research suggests that hearing voices may be shaped by local culture, there are also themes that seem to be common for many voice-hearers, across cultures. When I was working on *Living with Voices: 50 Stories of Recovery*, an anthology of testimonies from voice-hearers from all over the world, what struck me was that, even though each person's account was entirely unique, there were a number of key themes which emerged from all of the stories: that the voices were often a survival strategy, that the voices were deemed significant, decipherable, and intimately entwined to the hearer's life story, that voices sometimes used metaphorical language, and that healing was not contingent on banishing the voices but about understanding their meaning, improving communication with the voices, and, consequently, having a more positive relationship with them.

The acceptance of a diversity of explanations for hearing voices, which is a central tenet of the HVM, has been crucial in developing the HVM internationally, without trying to export and impose Western ideas and assumptions about the mind or human experience. The HVM stance is one of respectful curiosity about the myriad ways people have of understanding voices, visions, sensory experiences, and altered states of consciousness; we seek to support people to make sense of their experiences, on their own terms. So, despite the well-established link between hearing voices and traumatic and adverse life experiences, the HVM explicitly accepts all explanations for hearing voices which may include an array of belief systems, including the spiritual, religious, paranormal, technological, cultural, counter-cultural, philosophical, and medical. As well as this, research suggests that perhaps other, "non-Western" cultures have something to teach us about how to live more peacefully with voices.

EM: Can you tell us a little bit about your books Demedicalising Misery *and* Models of Madness?

JD: What both books have in common is that they challenge the simplistic, pessimistic, and often damaging theories of the biomedical model of mental health.

Demedicalising Misery (which I co-edited with critical psychiatrist Joanna Moncrieff and the critical psychologist, the late Mark Rapley) attempted to show that the modern conception of madness and misery as diseases, illnesses, or disorders that can only be understood within a specialist body of knowledge, fails to do justice to the range and meaning of these experiences. As well as that, such concepts obscure the features of modern society that make sanity a precarious state for many people; and that all too often, their encounters with psychiatric professionals transforms despair, withdrawal, disorientation, and distress into meaningless "illness."

Models of Madness (which I co-edited with psychologist John Read) also questions the assumptions underlying many of the dominant theories of mental health—that human misery and distress are caused by chemical imbalances and genetic predispositions—as propagated by the biomedical model. We cite an extensive body of research which shows that so-called hallucinations, delusions, and so on are best understood as reactions to adverse life events and that psychological and social approaches are safer and more effective than pharmacological interventions and electroshock treatment. We conclude with examining why such a damaging ideology has come to dominate mental health, why it persists, and how to change it.

EM: What are your thoughts on the current, dominant paradigm of diagnosing and treating mental disorders and the use of so-called psychiatric medication to treat mental disorders in children, teens, and adults?

JD: I think that the dominant paradigm of medicalizing people's suffering and the consequent proliferation of psychotropic medications is a deeply disturbing feature of modern life that urgently needs to be addressed. As it stands, most treatment is administered by people who are often well intentioned yet unaware of the contested nature of such conceptualizations of madness and distress. Frankly, I believe that it is a scandal that in the 21st century, intelligent people are expected to accept discredited diagnoses for fear of being labeled as "lacking in insight" and having treatment forced on them.

Every week, many thousands of people are coerced into taking medication that they don't want and which frequently does more harm than good. Every week, people are incarcerated against their will, detained under mental health legislation, "for their own good." Fighting for the rights of people deemed mentally ill, many who have already suffered more than enough, is the last great civil rights movement.

Thresholds of Chicago

Mark Furlong is the Chief Operating Officer at Thresholds in Chicago (see www.thresholds.org), Illinois's largest provider of community based, recovery focused services and supports for people experiencing mental health distress. He is a licensed clinical social worker in the state of Illinois. Over the last 30 years Mark has provided employment supports, homeless outreach, and housing support services. In 2004, he helped develop and launch the Thresholds Peer Success Center that is staffed entirely by people with a lived experience of recovery. Recently he has been involved in developing pilots to demonstrate that better insurance reimbursement structures can drive improved experience of care, better outcomes, and better use of limited resources.

Eric Maisel: Can you tell us a little bit about Thresholds?

Mark Furlong: Thresholds is Illinois's largest provider of community based rehabilitation and recovery services for people diagnosed with serious mental health conditions. Thresholds specializes in services that happen in the community, that is, beyond the four walls of an office or clinic. Thresholds was Illinois's first provider of assertive community treatment (ACT) and currently has over 100 teams providing various levels of supportive services for people diagnosed with mental health conditions.

Thresholds serves about 10,000 people per year in Chicago and north-eastern Illinois.

EM: Would you say that you have an underlying philosophy with regard to what helps people in distress?

MF: Thresholds held a round table discussion in 2012 where we asked a group of people who have recovered from serious mental health conditions what helped them. The themes that emerged in that round table reflect our philosophy about what helps.

1. Consider life as distinct from diagnosis;
2. Help meet basic needs;
3. Encourage empowerment;
4. Educate about how to manage conditions;
5. Support community;
6. Provide hope and encourage faith;
7. Teach healthy thinking;
8. Focus on wellness.

Mental health conditions have a lot in common with other health conditions. When a person experiences a serious and ongoing mental health condition, their life is changed. However, people can learn to manage these conditions to be able to live full and meaningful lives. There are a number of social determinants that affect a person's health and mental health. For example, without decent, safe housing, a strong social support network, and meaningful activities such as work or school, recovery from a mental health condition becomes more challenging.

When a person has a job, a good place to live, and relationships with people who believe that they can and will recover, the likelihood of them successfully managing a mental health condition increases greatly. At Thresholds, we place a great emphasis on housing, work, and belonging to a community that offers supportive relationships.

Another important factor is that people in distress will do much better when they drive their own recovery. At Thresholds, we spend a lot of time talking to people about their strengths, goals, dreams, and aspirations. The motivation to do the work necessary to manage a mental health condition has to come from a person's own desires. Nobody wants to do "mental health treatment." People just want to feel better and get on with living.

EM: *What are your thoughts about so-called psychiatric medication as it relates to the folks you serve?*

MF: Medication can be helpful in managing some mental health conditions but it is rarely sufficient by itself. The decision to take psychiatric medication should only be made after carefully weighing the risks and benefits. I know sometimes individuals and families can be desperate for relief from distressing symptoms and they are very happy for the symptom reduction that medication can provide. The problem is that many psychiatric medications are associated with long-term health risks and serious side effects.

Many people who have been diagnosed with schizophrenia or bipolar disorder decide to take medication for years. This is because they believe and have experienced that their lives are better when they take it. It's a very personal decision and at Thresholds we support people in making this decision.

EM: *If you had a loved one in emotional or mental distress, what would you suggest that he or she do or try?*

MF: That's a great question. Unfortunately, there is no simple or good answer to that question. The resources available in the US for people experiencing emotional or mental distress vary greatly at the state and community levels. Insurance coverage varies greatly as well. That said, I would recommend:

1. See your doctor for a good medical work up. There are a number of medical conditions that cause serious problems with mood or thinking.
2. See a counselor for an evaluation. If appropriate there are a number of evidence-based interventions that can be very helpful. You can search for "community mental health center" in your community or ask your physician or insurance company for a referral.
3. Find other people in your community who have gone through similar experiences. The support of a community can make a tremendous difference in a person's life. A counselor or community mental health center may be able to help you find these supports.
4. Learn about how diet, physical activity, sleep, stress, and other lifestyle factors affect your mental health. A lot of people experience relief by making changes in some of these factors.
5. If suicide or self-harm is a concern, call 9-1-1, a suicide hotline, or go to the closest emergency room.

MHALA Village

Mark Ragins is a psychiatrist who has been at the MHALA Village since it opened in 1990. He's worked on their Full Service Partnership teams, their Homeless Assistance Program, their Transitional Age Youth Academy, and now on their welcoming team and as their medical director. He's been heavily involved in the recovery movement for 25 years writing, speaking, training, consulting, and developing clinical and administrative tools to support their work.

Eric Maisel: Can you tell us a little bit about MHALA Village?

Mark Ragins: MHALA is a large local chapter of National Mental Health America. We operate a variety of programs centered around advocacy, public education, service delivery, innovation, workforce training, and community development. Our services are in two main clusters, one in Lancaster and one in Long Beach.

The Village was established in 1990 initially as a demonstration project funded by the California state legislature. Some of the same legislators who had brought deinstitutionalization to California in the 1970s had serious misgivings about how community mental health had turned out. Too many people seemed to be falling between the cracks and ending up not getting the help they needed. They wanted us to demonstrate the best that community mental health could be. They wanted us to "do whatever it took," including the clubhouse model, psychiatric rehabilitation, supported housing, education, employment, integrated substance abuse services, family support, crisis services, and facilitate health care—all in one integrated, "one-stop shop" program.

Administratively, we were integrated with capitated funding and quality of life outcome accountability. We soon found that the emerging recovery movement gave us the vision to integrate all those services into one welcoming, hopeful, vibrant program. The project's outside evaluator reported after three years that we had the best results across a range of quality of life outcomes of any program in the literature for people with a range of disabling mental illnesses.

Visitors began coming to the Village from all over the world to be inspired and instructed. We received a number of awards for our work. We became recognized leaders and proponents of the Recovery Model for people with mental illnesses. Over time we've adapted our methods to other specialized populations including homeless people, high utilizers, repeatedly hospitalized people, jail diversion, poorly engaged people, transitional-aged youth, veterans, and medically fragile homeless people.

Back at the Village, MHALA has moved from a "static" "services of indefinite duration" model to a "flow" model where people move along a continuum of recovery-based programs as they grow and recover. We now have a comprehensive recovery-based system of care in Long Beach. We designed the Milestones of Recovery (MORS) tool to track people's recovery and promote flow. We continue to innovate to improve our practice and push the boundaries of the recovery model while adapting to the ever-changing environment around us.

EM: Would you say that you have an underlying philosophy with regard to what helps people in distress?

MR: We believe in the recovery model of care. We believe that recovery isn't something that can be done to someone. It is a process where people overcome the losses and destruction in their lives to rebuild themselves, their relationships, and their roles in the community. Recovery is a path best traveled alongside a helpful guide or mentor.

We use four common stages of recovery (hope, empowerment, self-responsibility, and attaining meaningful roles) to help people live with dignity.

The three major transformations in the recovery movement are:

1. Person-centered: Moving from centering our efforts on the treatment of illnesses and the reduction of symptoms to a holistic service of people and the rebuilding of lives. This is needed to engage people.
2. Client driven/collaboration: Moving from professional directed relationships emphasizing informed compliance with prescribed treatments to individualized relationships emphasizing empowerment and building people's self-responsibility. This is needed to motivate and build skills.
3. Strengths based/resilience: Building hope for recovery upon each person's strengths, motivations, and learning from suffering rather than upon the competence of professionals and medications to reduce or eliminate the burden of their illnesses. This is needed to build self-reliance and move on from depending on professionals.

From the recovery model, we've created a set of practical principles we use to guide our work:

WE BELIEVE ...

1. Hope makes recovery possible; it facilitates healing of the mind, body, and spirit.
2. Welcoming people includes creating a culture of acceptance with easily accessible integrated supports and services.
3. Focusing on the whole person includes their strengths and weakness, abilities and barriers, wounds and gifts.
4. Each person creates their path and determines the pace of their recovery.

5. The recovery process is a collaborative journey in support of individuals pursuing their life goals.
6. Relationships are developed through mutual respect and reciprocity, including openness to genuine emotional connections.
7. A solid foundation for recovery is built by helping people to honestly and responsibly deal with their mental difficulties, substance abuse issues, and emotional problems.
8. People thrive, grow, and gain the courage to seek change in respectful environments that promote self-responsibility.
9. The practical work of recovery takes place in the community.
10. Each person has the right to fair and just treatment in their community ensured through advocacy and social responsibility.
11. Everyone deserves the opportunity to have a place to call home.
12. Promoting natural supports, having fun, and a sense of belonging enhances quality of life.
13. Employment and education are powerful means to help people build lives beyond their illness.
14. Program success is based on achieving quality of life and recovery outcomes.

EM: *If you had a loved one in emotional or mental distress, what would you suggest that he or she do or try?*

MR: We've too often come to a place where either people embrace the medical model entirely—searching endlessly for the perfect treatment, the right doctor or therapist, the right medication, the right hospital or program, and then turning themselves over to professionals to fix them, like it works on TV—or they reject medical treatment or even psychotherapy and try to recover on their own, or entirely within a counterculture. I don't think either extreme is the best option, but too often that's all that's available. Most of the people I've seen recover have integrated both professional treatment, often, but not necessarily including medications, with their own efforts to improve their lives. They've take self-responsibility for both their lives and their treatments.

Recovery-Oriented Approaches

Dr. Eleanor Longden is a researcher, mental health activist, and board member of Intervoice, currently based at The Psychosis Research Unit in

Manchester, England. She lectures and publishes internationally on the importance of emphasizing person-centered, psychosocial approaches to complex mental health problems. She is a former TED speaker and the author of Learning from the Voices in My Head.

Eric Maisel: Can you tell us a little bit about your story and your journey?

Eleanor Longden: When I was a teenager at university, I began hearing a single, neutral voice that calmly narrated everything I was doing in the third person: "She is going to a lecture." "She is leaving the building." Only the messages didn't stay passive for long. That day was the beginning of years of nightmarish voices, visions, and bizarre, terrifying delusions that drove me to self-harm in desperation, and led a psychiatrist to remark that I would have been better off with cancer because "it would be easier to cure than schizophrenia."

Essentially, I was diagnosed, drugged, and discarded by a system that didn't know how to help me. A major turning point was encountering individuals from the Hearing Voices Network, who were willing to acknowledge and understand the experiences of trauma and abuse I'd endured as a child and young adult, and how these horrors from the past were still being enacted in the present. It was a long, torturous journey, but once I started to interpret my terror and despair in terms of what I'd survived, I could begin to recover: that my so-called symptoms of schizophrenia weren't random products of a chemical imbalance but rather meaningful messages from my mind about the unbearable things I'd gone through.

I now have an exciting, enjoyable life as an academic and international speaker, have no contact with mental health services, and haven't taken medication for nearly 10 years. Although I still hear voices, I now accept them as part of myself. And just as I've come to terms with them—the experiences they represent and the messages they were trying to communicate—they have transformed in character. Today they are guides and allies, not tormentors.

EM: You advocate for "recovery-oriented approaches" to dealing with so-called serious mental illnesses and with trauma. What do you mean by a "recovery-oriented approach"?

EL: Recovery is a fundamental human right, and while there remains a great degree of pessimism about the capacity of people with "serious mental illness" to recover, the evidence shows that this is simply not true.

A recovery approach, from my perspective, is holistic, person-centered, solution-focused, and an ongoing journey rather than a fixed goal or endpoint. I think it's also very important to broaden the focus from clinical recovery to incorporate the concept of personal recovery: factors like hope, identity, empowerment, subjective meaning, and the ability to fulfill one's individual goals.

In my own personal journey, I spent many years stuck within the limitations of a coercive "cure" response, which emphasized factors like compliance, sedation, and silencing. In contrast, understanding, exploring, and engaging with the emotional meaning of my experiences was the recovery response. As Ron Coleman says, cure is something that's done to you—recovery you do for yourself.

For many of us, an important part of personal recovery is the transformative process of making sense of your experience on your own terms, and using this knowledge to guide and inform genuine healing and growth. Finally, it's also important that the concept of recovery is not used in a punitive or judgmental way. Complex factors like stigma, isolation, and hopelessness are major barriers to healing, and we need to recognize this and never blame someone for an inability to move forward in their recovery journey.

There should be a profusion of compassion, support, and material and emotional resources for those that need them; yet there should also always be hope. To quote Pat Deegan, another well-known figure in this field: "It's important to meet people where they're at, but not *leave them* where they're at."

EM: Can a person suffering from the sorts of emotional and mental distress currently called serious mental illness engage in this recovery work himself or herself or is outside or additional help needed?

EL: I think survivors must always be the authorities and authors of their own recovery process, but undoubtedly that journey becomes easier when you have allies to guide your way. There's a saying that it "takes a village to raise a child" and, in many ways, it takes a community to support a recovery story. For so many of us, the things that drive us mad, experiences of loss, trauma, discrimination, or injustice, take place on a silent, shameful, lonely stage. Recovery is the opposite: it's about reconnection and solidarity. This is why organizations like the Hearing Voices Movement can be so enormously empowering, because although they maintain an unshakable belief in the power and resilience of the individual, they also provide a place for shared support and mutual understanding.

Personally, I was extremely fortunate to have people who never gave up on me—relationships that really honored and acknowledged my resilience, my worth and humanity, and my capacity to heal. I used to say that these people saved me, but what I now know is that they did something even more important: they empowered me to save myself.

EM: If you had a loved one in emotional or mental distress, what would you suggest that he or she do or try?

EL: I probably wouldn't suggest anything initially, I'd just sit down and listen to their account of what's happening to them and how they're understanding it. I'd then make suggestions and offer choices, and do my best to try and help them find a way of navigating how they feel that makes sense to them.

My main priority in the short term would be looking for ways to help them feel safe and in control, both emotionally and physically, because safety is the foundation from which more long-term therapeutic work can begin. I'd also be aware that their needs and preferences could change as their journey progresses, so I would try to remain flexible in exploring things that might possibly help.

***

I hope that you found the above interviews suggestive and interesting. Even for a parent-client dealing with a child who is challenged by anomalous experiences like hearing voices, there are options available that are different from the current diagnose-and-treat-with-chemicals model and there are points of view different from conceptualizing what is going on as "disease." Your parent-client has much to explore and you can point her in those diverse directions.

10

WHAT YOU CAN OFFER

What exactly are you offering your parent-clients who are struggling with a distressed, disturbed, or "diagnosed" child? First of all, you are offering an attitude on inquiry. The current checklist system of diagnosing and treating mental disorders forecloses on investigation; but humane helpers know better than to engage in such premature foreclosing. They can approach their work with a spirit of inquiry and make the sorts of specific inquiries outlined in this book.

Helpers can support both their clients and their clients' children by providing clients with a better understanding of their parenting options and the resources available to them. They can likewise advocate both for their clients, who may feel pressured to accept the mental disorder paradigm, and for their clients' children, whose distress is likely to put them at risk of a mental disorder diagnosis and a chemical fix.

Helpers can likewise aid their clients in understanding the difference between reaching a diagnosis and affixing a label, and can further inform them about controversies regarding the DSM, which can legitimately be viewed as a shopping catalogue for labels and not a genuine diagnostic manual.

Without a humane helper's guidance, it can prove very hard for parents not to believe that something like medicine is going on when their child is diagnosed and prescribed psychiatric medication, since the analogy between "physical disorder" and "mental disorder" is a powerful one and since medical doctors are engaged in the diagnosing and the prescribing. Helpers can aid their parent-clients in understanding this.

You might also educate yourself a bit on what "testing" means in this context. What exactly is going on when a child is "tested" for something like "ADHD"? If your client's child is "tested" in some way and those results are used to "diagnose a mental disorder," your client will naturally be inclined to further believe in such a diagnosis. You can help her understand that the test in question needs to be valid in order for it to be trusted.

You might also invite your client to educate herself on the differences between medication and chemicals-with-powerful-effects, on the serious nature of the side effects of psychiatric medication, on the reality of the placebo effect, and on other aspects of the practice of "treating mental disorders with psychiatric medication."

In addition, you can help your client better understand that distress and difficulty are a part of life, that arbitrarily announcing how much distress or difficulty is "normal" is an illegitimate practice, and that difference (including differences in original personality) is not in and of itself a marker of abnormality or disease.

Jettisoning "Normal" and "Abnormal"

The matter of what is normal can't be and must not be a mere statistical nicety. It can't be and must not be "normal" to be a Christian just because 95% of your community is Christian. It can't be and must not be "normal" to be attracted to someone of the opposite sex just because 90% of the general population is heterosexual. It can't be and must not be "normal" to own slaves just because all the landowners in your state own slaves. "Normal" can't mean and must not mean "what we see all the time" or "what we see the most of." It must have a different meaning from that for it to mean anything of value to right-thinking people.

Nor can it mean "free of discomfort," as if "normal" were the equivalent of oblivious and you were somehow "abnormal" when you were sentient, human, and real. This, however, is the game currently being played by the mental health industry: it makes this precise, illegitimate switch. It announces that when you feel a certain level of discomfort, have certain anomalous experiences, or act in certain outsized ways you are abnormal and you have a disorder. It equates abnormal with unwanted, turning "I am feeling profoundly sad" into "You have the mental disorder of depression."

In this inappropriate view, "normal" is living free of excessive discomfort; "abnormal" is feeling or acting significantly distressed. Normal, in this view, is destroying a village in wartime and not experiencing anything afterward; abnormal is experiencing something afterward, and for a long time thereafter. The consequences of conscience, reason, and awareness are labeled abnormal and robotic allegiance to wearing a pasted-on smiley face is designated normal. Is that what we really mean? Is that what you believe "normal" and "abnormal" ought to mean?

Sadness, guilt, rage, disappointment, confusion, doubt, anxiety, and other similar experiences and states are all expected and normal, given the nature and demands of life; except, that is, to mental health professionals, where those states and experiences become markers of abnormality and cash cows. It is simply not right to call the absence of significant distress normal and the presence of significant distress abnormal. Does that seem right to you?

More than a hundred years of language analysis still hasn't helped us realize that the words we use matter. It is perhaps not in the nature of our species—not normal (wink, wink)—for a sufficient number of people to care enough about the terrible consequences of lame naming, consequences like forcing three, four, or five "normalizing" medications on a child. But we ought to care, because until we shed that unfortunate language we can't think very clearly about cause and effect in human affairs. And the subtleties of cause and effect ought to interest us!

Consider the following. Imagine five young boys growing up in the same group home where they are repeatedly and severely beaten. One grows up to be a ruthless businessman who makes a fortune. A second grows up to be a serial killer. A third grows up to be a repressed priest with a penchant for visiting discipline-and-bondage porn sites. A fourth grows up to be a loving family man afflicted with bad memories, stomach upsets, and difficulties concentrating. A fifth becomes a tortured poet who writes gorgeous, heart-felt poetry about pain and suffering and kills himself when he is 28.

Which of these are "normal" people and which of these are "abnormal" people? Which of these are "normal" outcomes and which of these are "abnormal" outcomes?

Do the words "normal" and "abnormal" help us at all or do they only get in the way of what we know to be true: that very different outcomes can arise from similar causes? Through a glass darkly, we see cause and effect at work here. The fingerprints of that seminal experience of brutality can be seen all over each outcome. We may despair about each of these outcomes: but that is not the same as saying that any one of them is "normal" or "abnormal." It is not like one of these five boys broke his arm and the other four didn't. All got broken. These outcomes make human sense.

When you fall from a tree and break your arm we say that you injured your arm. We do not call you abnormal. Can't we be that simple, sensible, and real with regard to sadness, psychological pain, overwhelm, anxiety, inner turmoil, and the other commonly occurring and understandable psychological events that members of our species face? Can't we stop calling them "symptoms of disease" and calling ourselves "abnormal" for experiencing them?

Isn't it time that we stopped being held sway by those mesmerizing forces that want us to avoid looking the reality of our human condition in the eye? If we could do that, if we could adopt a "new normal" that let quintessential human experiences into our definition of normal, we could begin to create a way of speaking and practical strategies, tactics, and plans that returned the tasks of living to those embroiled in living.

> "Normal" would now include pain, difficulty, and especially struggle. We would possess a "new normal" that caught up with our understanding of who we are and how we got here. If you believe that our species has evolved and was not created out of whole cloth, you should likewise realize that normal mental health aligns much more with the idea of struggle than with the idea of tranquility. We have evolved as a creature with roiling insides. To leave all that roiling, all that turmoil, all that sadness and pain out of our definition of normal mental health is to make a fundamental error.
>
> Why does a child sit at his desk as his teacher lectures? He sits there with his hands folded because he is coerced and socialized, not because he has any desire to be there. What is normal for him and what his being wants is to have him leap up and run off to play. What is normal for him are his squirming, his making faces, and his expressing his outrage at being forced to learn a list of Roman Emperors or Spanish Missions of California. He is struggling to sit there, not happy to sit there. If we do not honor that struggle as a feature of normal mental health we make a mockery out of the word normal.
>
> Either directly or between the lines, you can communicate this basic, essential idea to your parent-clients: that you are wary of using words like "normal" and "abnormal" and that it might serve them if they were wary, too.

You might also explain the following to your parent-clients. Each individual and each generation suffers from its particular challenges with respect to life purpose and meaning. Helpers can foster a better understanding of the existential challenges that their clients and their clients' children are facing by explaining certain key concepts, for example the difference between "life purpose" and "life purposes" and between "seeking meaning" and "making meaning." Whatever particular language you decide to use with regard to existential issues, chatting about such issues will deepen your conversations with your clients.

Whatever a helper's particular theoretical orientation, job description, or legal mandate may be, she will want to bring a psychological perspective to her work with her clients; and she will want to share that perspective with her clients, helping them understand that what is going on with or inside their child is quite likely psychological rather than medical in nature. And because these challenges are not likely medical in nature, unless they really are, then the language of medicine ought not to be used, especially the words "diagnosis" and "treatment."

The No-Labeling Alternative

The humane helper as I envision her would engage in no labeling whatsoever. It is wrong to "diagnose" someone because he hates his job, finds his subjects in school boring, becomes paralyzed in the face of hard choices, or is made severely anxious by his lack of success. These and a million similar human experiences are not "symptoms of mental disorders" or markers of biological breakage. They really should not be "diagnosed" as if a medical event was occurring or as if an observer knew what was going on inside the person.

What then are the alternatives to "diagnosis" if a person is coming to us for help? Well, we could ask him what seems to be wrong and he might tell us. The simplicity of this transaction may seem "simplistic" or "superficial"—but why should it seem that way? Why should it seem simplistic or superficial to ask a person what he thinks is wrong, listen to his answers, and maybe make some suggestions based on what he tells us? If he fibs and doesn't tell us the whole truth or even much of the truth, well, so be it. We will have to deal with that possibility in wise and crafty ways or else maybe we will have to sometimes just throw up our hands. But he might just tell us the truth and we might have some good advice for him. Why is that an outrageous idea?

In this human-sized scenario no "diagnosing" at all need go on. The straightforward alternative to "diagnosing" is not diagnosing and having a wise human interaction instead. Is this sort of simple, sensible interaction somehow just not fancy enough or "scientific" enough to warrant payment? Is it therefore anathema to mental health professionals?

If you are a mental health professional with objections to the current labeling scheme, you may nevertheless still believe that there must be some alternative system that will allow you to give reasonable names to what human beings present. You may deeply believe that there are ways to create a taxonomy that at least allows us to be able to say the equivalent of "A dolphin and a human being are both mammals." Mustn't something along those lines be possible? Can't we do even that minimal thing? That really remains to be seen—and the answer may prove to be no.

When there are a million possible causes of a thing like a smile or a sigh, we can either lump everyone who smiles together and lump everyone who sighs together, creating categories of "people who smile" and "people who sigh," or we can create a million individual "categories" for each person who smiles and for each person who sighs. Neither activity makes sense or is worth the effort. Rather, we are obliged to take all those sighs and all those smiles as part of what the person across from us presents and abstain from creating illegitimate or unnecessary categories. To create categories just for our own sake, so that we feel that we are doing something that resembles science, is to act in bad faith.

Imagine that one person is sad because he has no life purpose, another person is sad because his best friend is doing better than he is, a third person is sad because his mate is cheating on him, a fourth person is sad because he can't get over his childhood abuse, a fifth person is sad because he hates his government's policies, a sixth person is sad because winter has lasted eight months, a seventh person is sad because he can't get his novel written, an eighth person is sad because she has become invisible to men, a ninth person is sad because he can't find the wherewithal to announce his sexual orientation, and so on.

The "naming" alternatives here are to create the category of "sad people" (which is what we currently do by turning "sad" into the "mental disorder of depression") or to make all of the following categories: "people who are sad because their novel isn't working," "people who are sad because their mate is cheating on them," and so on. Is either naming operation useful or sensible? Is it useful to lump all sad people together under one umbrella?

Would it be sensible to create a million categories of sad people based on our guesses about what is making them sad? What would be the point to either naming operation?

Consider a second example. Imagine several unruly boys at a school. One is unruly because he is bored, a second is unruly because he is being picked on, a third is unruly because his parents fight all the time, a fourth is unruly to gain attention, a fifth is unruly because he's already a mean son-of-a-gun, a sixth is unruly because he finds math hard, and so on. To repeat, we can only do one of three things here with respect to naming. We can pin a single label on all these boys, using words like "defiant" or "oppositional" or "attention deficit disordered" and claiming that they all have the same "mental disorder." Or we can create a separate category for each "type of unruliness." Or we can admit that these boys really have nothing in common except one observable behavior. Either we create an empty category, endless categories, or no categories at all. Only the latter is honest.

Many professionals who oppose the current labeling system nevertheless believe that there must be some alternative labeling system that makes sense. Whether they want to retain the fancy word "diagnosis" or whether they are willing to give it up, they possess a belief that they can't shake that there must be some legitimate categories into which human beings fit. Aren't there really "hoarders" and "anorexics" and "alcoholics"? Aren't there really "pedophiles" and "cutters" and "schizophrenics"? Aren't these categories and many more like them reasonable, sensible, and useful categories? Isn't that just obvious?

No, it isn't—not at all. What if a "pedophile" is also an "alcoholic"? What if a "hoarder" is also a "schizophrenic"? What if someone is "anorexic," a "cutter," and also many other things as well, say "a fundamentalist," "an incest survivor," and a "classical musician." Which thing is she "really"? The idea that pinning a single label on a human being is reasonable, sensible, and useful breaks down the second you look closely at the idea. It may be very hard to shake your belief that we need labels like "clinical depression," "alcoholism," "anorexia," and so on; and yet shaking that belief is a necessary step if we are to effectively answer the question, "What should replace diagnosis?" The uncomfortable, even mindboggling answer is to not diagnose at all and to not create mere taxonomies of convenience.

Each person is his own story. No theory about him is true; no category into which you put him is a legitimate definition of him. This is the high ideal at the center of humanistic, existential, and person-centered therapy, that each person be considered a person, acknowledged as a person, and accepted as a person. What action plan flows from this way of thinking? I think a very simple one. The new slogan of our adept, updated, mental health professional might be, "We try to offer people the help they want and the help they need without labeling them." This might become one of your favorite slogans.

That isn't to say that we wouldn't need strategies and tactics. We would indubitably need tactics to deal with all the tricky ways that human beings behave. We would need tactics to deal with the person who refuses to eat, who starts drinking at dawn, who can't get on a plane, who feels sad every day. We would need lots of tactics! To say that we listen and respond is not to say that we are sitting in some easy chair. But to say that we need tactics is not to say that we need taxonomies. It adds nothing but an easy-to-use label to call the girl who refuses to eat "anorexic" or the man who starts drinking at dawn "alcoholic."

Helpers need tactics and not taxonomies. You should think of yourself as a tactician and not a diagnostician. When you sit across from a person and you want to help him, you don't need to know what to call him. You need to know what to do to help him. The place for diagnosing and treating is medicine—or car repair, for that matter. When it comes to the emotional and mental health of human beings, we must refrain from pinning labels on them just because we can. As far as that goes, we could label everyone. And that would help no one except those who profit from labeling.

In addition to the above, helpers will want to do all of the following.

Listening, Hearing, and Wondering

If your client tells you in passing that her son has recently begun sharing a room with his older brother, moved into an accelerated program at school, or was demoted to second string on his high school football team, you want to hear that news and then wonder aloud about whether those changes may be contributing to or even causing her son's current problems.

You do not need to act like you know for certain that these changed circumstances matter or even that you suspect that these changed circumstances matter. All you need to do is wonder aloud and create an opening for your client to wonder, too. It may not have crossed her mind that sharing a room, getting into a tougher academic program, or losing prestige at school might negatively and even dramatically affect her son's emotional health. Now, hearing from you that events of this sort are worth thinking about, she can make use of the space and time you give her to think about them.

Summarizing

Say that you are talking with your client about her son's anger, recent diagnosis of ADHD, and new regimen of psychiatric drugs. After you've chatted a bit, or near the end of the session, you might summarize your client's options or possible next steps, including both those that she mentioned in session and some that you take it upon yourself to mention. This sort of summarizing is a lot of work and, insofar as you are adding suggestions of your own, quite directive and opinionated. But it can also prove enormously helpful. Your client will be much better able to follow up if you offer her this point-by-point summarizing.

Refrain from Using Mental Disorder Language

If you agree that mental disorder language is misguided and unhelpful at best and unscientific and illegitimate at worst, you will be careful not to use it. You will be careful not to start sentences with "Since your son has ADHD," "Since your daughter is schizophrenic" or "Since your son is an addict." But what about "Since your daughter is depressed"? Isn't it a bit awkward to say "Since your daughter is so sad" or "Since your daughter is in despair" rather than the more usual "Since your daughter is depressed"? Yes, it is awkward; but it is also better. Since the word "depression" has both an everyday sense and a mental disorder sense, and since the two are continually conflated, it is better to drop even "depression" from your vocabulary.

Of course, this can make communicating more difficult, more awkward, more confusing, and even a bit tortured. It may force you to have to repeatedly explain why you do not believe in mental disorder language and why, therefore, you are refraining from using it. But it is nevertheless important that you do refrain. By refraining, you are providing your client with tremendous help, because you are helping her to understand that what is going on with her child ought not to be considered a medical situation (unless it really is).

Shift to a "Problems in Living" Mindset

Make the shift in your own mind from "mental disease thinking" to "problems in living thinking." Rather than automatically ticking off squirming as a "symptom" of the "mental disorder of ADHD" or gloominess as a "symptom" of the "mental disorder of clinical depression," train yourself to ask yourself the question, "I wonder why little Johnny is squirming?" or "I wonder why Jane is gloomy?" Lead with "What's going on?" rather than with "What mental disorder can I detect?" Stop looking for mental disorders just because a shopping catalogue for mental disorders, the DSM, happens to exist and happens to have been foisted upon you.

This may not prove a shift that you can accomplish easily or overnight, especially if your interactions with colleagues, HMOs, and even friends and family pull at you to retain a "disorder label" way of talking. What will you say if your cousin announces that his young son has some new sensitivity mental disorder and asks what you think about whether he should be accommodated or mainstreamed in school? It is going to prove very hard, verging on impossible, not to put on your professional face and collude in acting like this new sensitivity mental disorder exists and is a real thing. It is one thing to change your own mind about mental disease thinking and as an abstract matter decide to repudiate it; it is a rather more difficult task to make that change when you talk to other people.

Allow Yourself to Look (and Be) Human

Make the shift from "I need to look like an expert" to "I need to be human." You entered a helping profession for many reasons but among them was the desire to look like an expert, to be accorded the material and psychological perks that professionals receive, and to have your ego massaged by being called "doctor" or "counselor" or something similar.

It isn't that you need to apologize for the fact that you aren't really doing medicine or announce that you aren't really a professional. Rather this shift is internal, away from acting like you know (which is the stance we want from our plumber, lawyer, or accountant) and toward the attitude of experimentalist, one who, like any scientist, has tools, tactics, tricks, and ideas but who, for example, doesn't really know what transpired before the big bang occurred until he really does know. A plumber's job is to fix broken pipes; a scientist asks questions. You can still be the professional you want to be: just shift away from plumber and toward scientist.

Deeply Accept Not Knowing

Shift toward a deep acceptance of the fact that you don't really know what's going on in and with the person sitting across from you, that you do not know what is going on in or with her distressed child, and become much easier with all that not knowing. Admit out loud that you don't know; that the two of you are guessing; and that your suggestions are more like experiments that may prove fruitful than like expert advice that comes with guarantees. At the same time remember that all this not knowing doesn't mean that you don't have ideas about what might help and tactics and strategies for helping.

Indeed, despite all that not knowing you do know a lot and have a lot to offer. You have a spirit of inquiry to share, support to provide, a dialogic method that helps clients express their feelings and communicate their issues, and information to share. That you do not know what is "really going on" doesn't lead to the conclusion that you don't have help to offer.

Coaching Vignettes

Consider the following vignettes from my coaching practice. I work primarily with creative and performing artists in a coaching capacity (I used to work with them as a family therapist and a psychotherapist). What follows are six brief vignettes from my practice, to give you a sense of how you can make use of the ideas I've been presenting.

Marjorie

My client Marjorie was a singer with a day job. Her husband also worked, which meant that they'd had to find a nanny for their almost-two-year-old daughter Jenny. Marjorie and I were working on moving her singing career forward as our main coaching goal, but in session she made mention of the fact that Jenny seemed very despondent, cried easily and apparently for no reason, and just didn't seem like herself. She wondered if Jenny, a sweet, sensitive girl, might be suffering from childhood depression.

I wondered aloud if Marjorie perhaps had any ideas about what might be going on? Were there any changed circumstances? Anything new or different happening that she could put her finger on? Anything perhaps traumatic going on in Jenny's life? Marjorie confessed that she and her husband had been fighting a bit but that they were careful to keep that bickering as far away from Jenny as possible. Marjorie wondered if perhaps Jenny was in fact getting wind of that somehow and was reacting to their acrimony? I agreed that that was certainly possible.

Then I had a thought. "What about the nanny?" I wondered. "Is she nice to Jenny?"

"She's perfect," Marjorie replied. "The best."

I was well aware of nannies who "looked perfect" when the parents were around but who could be mean and cruel as soon as they left. I didn't say that; but I did propose that Jenny engage in a little investigating.

"Does the nanny take Jenny anywhere where you have friends or acquaintances?"

"The library," Jenny replied. "Just about every day."

"Ask one of those friends or acquaintances for her truthful opinion about how the nanny is with Jenny. It can't hurt to check, can it?"

"All right," Marjorie agreed reluctantly. "But I think she's great."

The next time we spoke, Marjorie was in a state.

"You were right!" she exclaimed. "Apparently Maria has been mean to Jenny all along, yanking her hard by the arm, getting right in her face in the nastiest way—just being cruel. God! We had zero idea!"

They fired Maria and hired a new nanny. A few months later Marjorie reported that Jenny was like a new person—or like her happy, smiling, outgoing old self. Marjorie got lucky that I happened to have a wonder, that she played along with my wonder, and that we accidentally landed on the actual problem. But she only got lucky because I didn't immediately go down the road of presuming that Jenny had something called "childhood depression." Rather, I wondered aloud about what might be going on. You, too, can wonder aloud.

Leslie

Leslie, a painter, came to see me because she'd stopped painting. She had a taxing day job and two small children at home, a four-year-old boy and a two-year-old daughter, whom her stay-at-home partner watched. Leslie's day consisted of a chaotic morning routine, a commute, her day job, a commute home, and a further round of chores and dramas. No wonder that she wasn't painting!

She complained that her four-year-old, Barry, was subject to really monumental melt-downs. The smallest thing could set him off on an uncontrollable tantrum and, to use Leslie's language which no doubt she had picked up from the zeitgeist, make him "defiant" and "oppositional." Instead of walking with her down that route, I said, "Can you kind of predict what sorts of things will set Barry off?"

"Yes. If you touch his action figures and put one of them out of place. If we give the two-year-old a treat before we give Barry his. If we do anything outside of his normal routine, especially his bedtime routine. And if he himself does something that upsets him, like make his 'B' backwards or spill something on 'the book' he's writing. He's always writing 'a book.'"

I smiled. "So, some of the things are in your control, like giving him the treat first and not touching his action figures, and some aren't."

"Yes. But why should he always get the treat first? How is that fair?"

"Maybe 'fair' isn't quite the issue," I wondered. "Maybe this is a completely understandable developmental stage in the life of a bright, sensitive, creative boy and maybe just living with it is the answer. What do you think about maybe making just a few changes, like indulging him in getting his treat first, but otherwise basically putting up with it for another six months and see if it passes?"

"You don't think he has oppositional defiant disorder?"

I smiled again. "Or is he a bright, sensitive, creative boy at an awkward age?"

Leslie laughed. "Let's go with that."

Over time, Leslie resumed her painting career; and, as Barry approached his fifth birthday, his outbursts became so occasional that all Leslie could say about him was, "He's just the sweetest boy."

Bob

Bob, an academic, came to see me because he couldn't seem to motivate himself to finish the book he'd been working on for more than three years. At some point, he mentioned that his seven-year-old daughter Sophia was acting highly anxious. He feared that she might have an "anxiety disorder." What did I think?

"Are you anxious?" I asked.

"Yes. We've talked about that."

"Is your wife anxious?"

"Yes."

"Do either of you much like social situations?"

"God, no!"

"Then it appears that your daughter is your child," I said.

He thought about that.

"Are you saying it's genetic?"

"No."

"Are you saying that there's nothing to be done?"

"No. We've talked about anxiety management techniques for you. Have you tried them out?"

"The one about 'flipping the calmness switch.' I have tried that. And it's done a lot of good."

"Then that's the model, don't you think? See if Sophia can identify which particular things are making her anxious. Maybe she can. And maybe some of those can be changed. But even if she can't perfectly identify why she's feeling anxious, she can still be helped to learn some techniques. Don't you think?"

"That makes sense."

"Have a quiet conversation with her. That's the first step."

"And not look into anxiety medication?"

"What do you think?"

He thought about that. "No, not yet."

Julia

Julia, an actress, came to see me because she was trying to decide whether or not she should fire her agent, whether or not she should move to New York, whether or not she should accept any more roles in student productions, and many other career-related questions. At some point, she announced the following about her nine-year-old son Jonathan.

"He has ADHD, just like me," she said. "I've had him tested. Now we know for sure."

"That he has a mental disorder?"

"No, that he has ADHD."

"That's a mental disorder diagnosis. You believe he has a mental disorder?"

"No! He has ADHD."

"Then you're saying that he has a mental disorder. And, according to you, that you do as well."

"No! We're just different from other people! We don't have mental disorders."

"Then neither of you has ADHD."

The next time we met, Julia said, "I've been reading up on ADHD. Jonathan's the youngest kid in his class by several months. That may be the whole thing."

"Or at least a lot of it," I agreed.

Marcia

Marcia was a highly successful romance writer who came to see me because she'd stopped writing, apparently because her husband belittled her genre and invariably threw cold water on her successes. It also came up that her eleven-year-old daughter Andrea had begun to hide out in her room, where she could be heard sobbing. Marcia had tried to talk with Andrea and find out what was going on, but Andrea couldn't or wouldn't say. Marcia thought that it was perhaps time for Andrea to visit a psychiatrist, so as to be diagnosed with what Marcia presumed must be depression.

"How does your husband treat Andrea?" I asked.

"The same way he treats me."

"Is that okay?"

Marcia grew tearful. "No. It's one thing how he treats me. But he shouldn't treat Andrea that way."

"He shouldn't treat either of you that way."

"No, of course. But with me ... I'm part of the problem, putting up with it. Andrea hasn't done anything."

"And?"

A year later she and her husband were divorced. Marcia helped Andrea connect up with both a mentor and a supportive psychotherapist and, while Andrea couldn't be said to be happy, she did look to be on the mend.

Arnold

Arnold was a successful sculptor who came to see me because he was toying with the idea of starting to paint and wondered if that was a good idea or a terrible idea. His sculptures had begun to bore him, he had some painting ideas that excited him, and his wife, who ran the business end, told him that he was crazy to contemplate such a switch, which she characterized as "super-indulgent."

During a session, the tribulations of his seventeen-year-old son came up for the first time.

"Robert is using cocaine," Arnold said.

I nodded.

"Worse than that. He's selling it. He got arrested."

It turned out that rather than throwing the book at him, the judge Robert got offered him the choice between juvenile hall or a diversion program.

"He's refusing the diversion program!" Arnold exploded. "Because he 'doesn't have a problem with cocaine.' He's going to choose jail over diversion just so that he won't have to admit that he's an addict!"

"Are there a variety of diversion programs he can choose from or just one court-mandated one?"

"No, there are lots, just so long as they meet certain criteria."

"And he's refusing them all?"

Arnold hesitated. "No. There's one wilderness therapeutic camp that he's willing to go to, but it costs a fortune."

"And you couldn't raise that from family?"

"I couldn't let anyone in the family know!"

I paused. "No? You're furious at him for not admitting that he has a problem but you're unwilling to admit to your family that he has a problem?"

Arnold sat with that. In the end, he continued sculpting, so as to maximize his income; he confided in an uncle, who loaned him the money for Robert's wilderness camp; and after many dramas and refusals, Robert went to the camp, which experience made a real difference in his life.

***

My work with these six clients did not primarily focus on their children's troubles. Nor is your work with your parent-clients likely to primarily focus in that way. It's more likely that any such issues will come up in passing and will not amount to your main work together. But that they only come up in passing and that they don't amount to your main work together doesn't mean that those issues aren't important. Nor does it mean that you aren't helping—perhaps a great deal—by willingly engaging in such conversations and by offering your parent-clients a vision different from the currently dominant diagnose-and-treat-with-chemicals paradigm.

11

WHAT PARENTS CAN DO

In the next chapter, I'll provide you with 31 questions that you can give to your parent-clients for their consideration and/or that you can use as a personal reference to remind you what issues confront parents today. In this chapter, I want to provide you with some tips for parents, which you can share with your parent-clients, either in a hand-out sort of way or as part of the conversations you have with them.

> **Top 10 Tips for Parenting**
>
> Tim Carey is a Professor and Director of Flinders University's Centre for Remote Health in Alice Springs, Australia. He is a clinical psychologist, researcher, supervisor, teacher, and trainer. Tim has over 100 publications including books, book chapters, and journal publications. He has also developed a personalized psychotherapy called the Method of Levels (www.methodoflevels.com.au). Tim explained:

I'm usually pretty uncomfortable about giving advice and suggestions to other people. The things that I find helpful from my perspective, to live the life I want, are not necessarily going to be helpful for others to live the life they have in mind. With that caveat out of the way, I think parenting is a unique privilege and perhaps the single most important role in society. I've found the principles from Perceptual Control Theory to be of enormous assistance in thinking through ways to build strong, stable, and contented family relationships. From these principles, I've gleaned some ideas that may be of interest to you.

To reconcile my difficulty with giving advice, I've framed these "tips" as questions to invite you to reflect on your role as a parent. Through this reflection you might have the opportunity to consider the extent to which the way you are currently parenting measures up to the parent you would most like to be. I read these questions out to my 10-year-old son to seek his opinion as to their value. He said "They are good. Reading them you could really get some good ideas about how to be a better parent."

Here are the questions with some explanatory sentences and additional questions accompanying them. You'll notice as you read through the information that there are common themes and even some overlap in the explanations provided with each topic question. There is a great deal of convergence in many of these ideas but arbitrarily dividing them into 10 separate topics might help to illustrate them in different ways so that one or more of the explanations might make sense to you.

1. *Is parenting a priority?* To what extent do you think about parenting as your most important job? Is parenting something you make time for or does it routinely get relegated to the bench while you attend to other things such as work commitments, going to the gym, or a weekend away with the girls or boys? It's definitely important to maintain a balance in your life and looking after yourself is essential. When there is a choice to be made, though, how often does parenting win out? If your favorite TV show comes on just at the time your child wants to hear a bedtime story, what do you do? To what extent did your

life change after becoming a parent or is parenting something you fitted into the life you had created before you became a parent?
2. *What are your parenting goals?* When I read this question to my son, he said "You should know what you want to achieve by being a parent." I couldn't put it any better. What do you want to achieve as a parent? In 30 years' time, what memories do you want to have of "right now" and the time you spent with your children? What memories do you want your children to have? In many parenting programs there is a strong emphasis on the child's behavior and things parents can do to shape or guide this behavior. What about your own behavior? How much of the time do you spend being the parent you want to be?
3. *How often do you let them be?* "Letting them be" isn't necessarily the same as ignoring them or leaving them alone. Where practical, though, to what extent do you provide your children with the space to learn and grow and develop and find out about themselves? Are the young people you parent able to choose the clothes they wear? Can they make their own decisions about how much food they put on their plate from the dietary options you provide? How is bedtime decided? If we left a voice recorder in your house for a day, what would we hear? Is your communication with your child characterized by instructions and commands or do you convey a sense of intrigue and wonder at discovering the person who is "becoming" right before your eyes?
4. *How strong are your relationships?* How often do you spend time just hanging out and having fun with your child? Are there activities you both find enjoyable that you do together on a regular basis? Is your child someone you enjoy spending time with or would you rather find other things to do? Whenever there are difficulties, and there will always be difficulties, your ability to resolve these difficulties successfully may very well hinge on the strength of your relationship.
5. *Do you admit it when you're wrong?* No one gets it right all the time. Many children have a strong sense of justice and fair play. How do you handle situations when you've got it wrong? Do you believe that, as a parent, it's important not to show

weakness and not to admit that you're wrong? What might your children be learning from the expression of a belief like this?

6. *Do you reflect the qualities you want your children to value?* When I read this out to my son, he said "Does this mean 'Are you a good role model?'" Once again, I think he nailed it. Do you value cooperation? If you do, how often do you cooperate with your child on things where they would like you to cooperate? Do you value honesty? Are you honest with your children? Children seem to learn far more by the sort of person we are than by what we directly set out to teach them. When plans go awry, how do your children see you respond?

7. *Do you know your children?* Do you know what your children like and don't like? Do they have goals that are important to them? How do you and your children spend your time together? Do you discuss things with them and seek their ideas and opinions? From the very beginning people have preferences about the way they like things to be. As we grow and learn, these preferences can expand and become more sophisticated. Preferences can also change with new experiences. Do you ever find yourself saying to your child "But you always used to like X"? How well are you keeping up with your child's changing priorities and values?

8. *To what extent do you ask questions rather than giving commands and instructions?* There is certainly room for both questions and instructions in the course of routine parent–child communication. If you pay attention, however, it's likely to be the case that the proportion of instructions you issue far outweigh the amount of questions you ask. There are countless opportunities when children and young people could be asked rather than told. For example, rather than saying "Get your coat before we leave the house" you could say "Are you wearing everything you need before we go out?" or "When you look at the weather outside, what clothes do you think you'll need?" Asking questions encourages children to think about things in a way that giving instructions doesn't. It's important though, to avoid asking questions rhetorically. Rhetorical questions are not that different from instructions. A useful guideline with

which to reflect on your questioning style is to consider whether you would ask questions of another adult, your partner perhaps or a friend, in the same way you ask them of your child.

9. *How much fun do you have with your children?* In the hustle and bustle of daily living we can get caught up in routines, deadlines, and appointments and not pay enough attention to just enjoying the other people we are building a life with. How often have you had a good belly laugh with your children? Have you ever done silly things together? Do you ever spend nights playing games rather than watching the television, posting on Facebook, or answering emails? In years to come, your children might not remember how many friends you had on Facebook but they might reminisce fondly about the times you tickled each other or built a pirate ship together.

10. *How does your child experience you?* If you spend time wondering about the world as your child experiences it, what would your best guess be about how your child views family living? We can never know this with certainty of course but it can be a useful thought exercise nevertheless. Are your children's daily lives characterized by closeness, conversation, camaraderie, and compassion? Or would their experience be more about being directed, instructed, and ordered around? Would they describe you as stern and strict? Is that the way you want them to describe you? How would you like them to think of you? Are the experiences you present them with on a daily basis consistent with the way you want them to experience you as a parent?

Now that I've outlined my 10 top tips and provided a little explanation with each one, perhaps you'll find something useful in the ideas I've discussed. The more you can recognize that your children are trying to make their worlds be the way they want them to be just as you are, the more you might be able to find creative and enjoyable ways to live harmoniously together. Parenting is the greatest trip on earth. I wish you the ride of your life.

The above are what might be called general parenting skills. In addition to these, parents also need to be skillful when it comes to the various issues that arise at different stages of child development (e.g. dealing skillfully with a toddler who's biting, a three-year-old who's going off to preschool for the first time, an older child who's growing restless or defiant at school or at home). That is, in addition to a loving attitude, a respect for your child, and other basics, there are many tactics and strategies to acquire to help deal with the many specific (and often predictable) issues that arise.

Parenting a So-Called "ODD Kid"

Maureen Healy is an award-winning author, popular speaker, and leader in the field of children's emotional health. Her mentoring program for highly sensitive children has helped parents and their children worldwide. To learn more see: www.growinghappykids.com. Maureen explained:

Many children are uncooperative, defiant, and argumentative, especially towards people in authority like parents and teachers. Oftentimes when we're faced with a child who refuses to participate in the classroom or complete their homework, we get angered. But if we can keep the lid on ourselves, perhaps one of the following tips can help you calm and connect with your child on the path to more ease.

1. *Listen*. The number one situation I see is that children diagnosed with ODD [oppositional defiant disorder] feel grossly misunderstood and once they're better understood their need for defiance goes way down. Said differently, if you as the parent or teacher can learn what they're so angry about or triggered by, then you can help them move in a more positive direction by emotionally connecting with them (empathy) and redirecting them. Without this step, there is little hope for progress.

2. *Partner with Your Child*. Everything about teaching and parenting is about partnering with children these days. Gone are the days where authoritative approaches were rewarded or frankly

worked. Today, we need to work together and problem solve. I'm not saying that you let your son or daughter run the house because there are things that are non-negotiable (e.g. showering or bathing, doing homework, changing underwear) but how things get done usually has a great deal of flexibility. For example, do you want to do your homework now, in two hours, or before you leave in the morning for school? Providing options reduces conflict.

3. *Praise Small Steps of Cooperation.* Every step forward needs praise, even if it feels ridiculous, especially if we're doing our best to change behavior or automatic responses. For example, say your son, Marcus, gets into the minivan and for the first time doesn't say, "I don't want to go there," but instead cooperates. Boom, thank him and recognize his ability to go with the flow.

4. *Focus on Problem-Solving.* Defiant children get angry easily and their default position is: "No, I will not do my homework" or "No, I'm not going to that birthday party!" So, regardless of the situation, it's usually helpful to invite your son or daughter to help solve the problem. For example, with the homework, you might ask: "What would you need to complete your homework? Or is there another creative way we can do it?" Billy, aged 10, hated writing book reports, so his dad, Fred, bought him an audio software program that helped him complete the assignment in a way that worked for him. That's an example of the sort of problem-solving I have in mind.

5. *Still Love When You're Not Feeling Loving.* Remember that the kids who are the hardest to love are the ones who need it the most. This doesn't need much explanation, but it's a motto of mine.

6. *Find What Motivates Them.* Use what motivates your child to inspire him. Every being on the planet is motivated either internally, externally, or a combination of both. Boys and girls with a diagnosis of ODD are often not externally motivated by punishments or by pressure to cooperate, so it takes some sleuthing to discover what really is driving them—but when you do, you can help motivate and inspire them to cooperate because you've find their driving force. For example, Mattie

loves money, which sounds silly at age eight, but he does. If you pay him to do something, whether it's take the trash out or make breakfast for his siblings, he does it happily even for a few quarters. Try to be creative in your hunt for what will motivate your child.

7. *Get Your Child a Mentor.* Parents are in the hardest role, tasked with caring for their children, keeping them safe, and doing their best to have fun with them despite the challenges of everyday living. One of the reasons I started my mentoring program for highly sensitive children is because having an outside person guide your child in the direction of positive emotional health and teach them tools to help them move in a positive direction is very effective. Often it doesn't take much for a child to start making positive shifts, but it can be speeded up with a mentor's help.

8. *Get Someone to Translate Your Child's Language or Behavior.* Find someone who is "cut from the same cloth" as your child but who has learned how to make their defiant tendencies a strength versus a liability. This is why I mentor highly sensitive children, because I was one.

9. *Teach Why Teamwork Matters.* Many children don't inherently value working together. It's almost like they don't trust others or see the point. Helping children realize that we can do more as a team than alone is a valuable part of the "cure" of so-called ODD. For example, think Sheldon Cooper from the popular television series, *The Big Bang Theory.* It's easy to think of this mathematical genius as not only defiant but uncooperative. Actually, I've seen research that many children with so-called ODD are gifted and I bet that their oppositional nature was given to them as a gift; but helping them make it so is our work.

10. *Remember That You May Be Parenting a Leader.* You're probably parenting a leader so think of it as an extra-credit assignment from God. The question is: How do you lead a leader? This is the billion-dollar question without any exact answer; but helping your child gain a good character and decision-making abilities, as well as bolstering their social and emotional health, is going to put them on the right path. And don't forget that you don't need

> to do it alone—build a team around them, whether that's a therapist, a mentor like me, someone in your community, or someone in your child's school. The success of your child doesn't just rest on you—it rests on all of us.

In addition to honing general parenting skills and acquiring tactics and strategies to deal with specific issues, parents will also want to learn basic life skills. These skills include managing anxiety and practicing calmness, manifesting courage and strength, bringing awareness and clarity to situations, and learning how to be really present rather than absent or scattered.

Take the basic life skill of presence. In order to effectively deal with difficult family situations, you need to "be here now." You need to be present so that you can muster your strength, your courage, your clarity, your smarts, and your other skills and attributes. If you're only half-here, you're unlikely to find the motivation, the serenity, or the inner resources to cope. What makes any difficult family situation all the more difficult is how hard it is to actually be present. Most people are not "here right now." Rather, they are elsewhere, distracted by their noisy thoughts and their racing emotions.

If, for example, you have some time available and it is important that you have a certain difficult conversation with your teenage son, then it is not being present to do some other "reasonable" thing during that period of time, something like weeding your garden, planning your menus for the week, catching up on the world news, or making sure that the storm windows are in good working order. You could make a case for the reasonableness of any of those activities—but not in this context. In this context, they must be seen as ways that you are avoiding having that difficult conversation with your son: that is, seen as ways to be absent.

Doing those things would amount to avoidance. So, too, would thinking about those things. It isn't useful during that time period to think about weeding your garden, planning your menus for the week, catching up on the world news, or examining your storm windows, not if what you ought to be thinking about is what to say to your son. In this set of circumstances, thoughts about weeds and menus are deflections and distractions. They are thoughts that only help you avoid the hard work of dealing with your teenage son.

If, on the other hand, you managed to be present, you might instead rehearse what you wanted to say to your son and rehearse your responses to his denials and justifications; you might research some information on the Internet relevant to your son's situation; you might practice an anxiety management technique in anticipation of your upcoming stressful conversation; or you might quiet yourself, center yourself, and march right off to find your son and talk to him. It is fine to weed the garden or to think about weeding the garden—just not if right now you ought to be dealing with your son's problem.

On top of our defensiveness and our desire to distract ourselves from the important business at hand, a second challenge harms our ability to be present. That is the way that the past intrudes upon the present. We know that it would serve us to think clearly about what might best help our son and what precisely we want to say to him; we try to do exactly that; and instead of being able to focus on those important tasks we find ourselves flooded with anguish about the past, filled with regrets about how we let our son down over the years, or saddened by our past wrong turns and mistakes. Those unwanted, intrusive thoughts prevent us from being here right now. Suddenly we are remembering—and stewing about—something we did or failed to do 20 years ago; and we are left with no mind space to deal with our son's current pressing situation.

These two challenges, dealing with our defensive distractibility and dealing with the past unceremoniously returning, amount to lifelong challenges. How can we deal with them? We can make an effort to deal with them by holding the intention to "be here now," by maintaining awareness about our very human penchant to fool ourselves, trick ourselves, and distract ourselves, by practicing calmness and thus reducing the anxiety that causes us to want to distract ourselves and flee, by engaging in a regular practice (like a meditation practice) whose objective is to teach us how to "be here now," and by enacting ceremonies that help keep us present.

We may never get perfect about being present—but we can make many improvements and giant progress.

With respect to your defensive distractibility, you might try the following. Think about something that you find difficult to think about—in the example I've been using, that difficult conversation you know that you need to have with your son. As you try to engage with that difficult subject matter, notice where your thoughts want to go. Do they go to the past and regrets? Do they go to some task that suddenly seems very important to consider, like weeding your garden? Wherever they go, calmly but firmly say, "I need to come back to what's really important." Maybe that precise phrase won't work so well for you; if it doesn't, then pick a phrase that does. Practice this exercise and see if you can gain some mastery over your wandering thoughts.

What if the past keeps returning? Say, for example, that certain regrets keep coming back to haunt you. Maybe you regret the wrong paths you took, the time you wasted, the opportunities you missed, the ways in which you failed yourself or failed others—and those regrets keep coming back with a vengeance. What might you try? The following is a powerful ceremony that I often present at my writing workshops to help writers heal their regrets. You might give it a try.

In addition to the regrets that we all harbor, writers harbor many additional ones: for example, that they haven't produced writing of a consistently high quality, that they haven't written as often or as much as they should have, or that they haven't had the publishing successes they dreamed of having. I have them choose one of those poignant regrets, write it down on a sheet of paper, fold up the paper, tear the paper to shreds, and toss the shreds in the air while saying or thinking, "I am through with that regret!" You might give this very useful ceremony a try.

It is hard to be present and it is doubly hard to be present in the face of difficulty. We are as much designed to flee as to stay put. Nor is focusing single-mindedly on something—focusing on the potato we are peeling as we peel it—being present in the sense we are discussing. Rather, you need to be present to what you need to do, not just present to the activity in which you are engaged. If what you really need to do right now is have a certain difficult conversation with your son, being present to that reality means being present to it and not to the potato you are peeling, the regrets you are feeling, or your garden that needs weeding. By being present I mean something that sets the bar very high: being present to that which really requires your attention.

Some parents will be dealing with a child who is in what feels to the parent like an extreme state (it may or may not feel that way to the child). One classic extreme state is "hearing voices." If your child is experiencing auditory or visual hallucinations, that may feel scary beyond belief. Even with respect to such extreme states, there are parenting skills to learn. Consider, for example, what researchers on "The Young Voices" study have learned.

> ### The Young Voices Study: Advice for Parents from Parents
>
> *Dr. Sarah Parry is a Clinical Psychologist, Senior Lecturer in Clinical and Counselling Psychology at Manchester Metropolitan University, and head of the team that is researching "The Young Voices" study. Sarah explained:*
>
> Over recent months, we have been hearing from young people who hear voices and their parents/guardians. As we discussed in a recent article in *The Conversation UK*, hearing voices is by no means unusual during childhood and an experience that some young people find helpful and comforting in times of stress and difficulty.
>
> As well as talking to young people, we have heard from parents from the UK, Norway, and Australia about their experiences of supporting their children, seeking help from health services, and how they have come to make sense of the voices their children hear. Although our study is still in the early stages, the responses we have had from our online parent survey have been incredibly helpful and full of useful recommendations and insights.
>
> (The online surveys for parents are available at www.mmu.ac.uk/hearing-voices-parents and for young people who hear voices at www.mmu.ac.uk/hearing-voices-children.)
>
> #### *Top 10 Tips from Parents*
>
> 1. *Don't panic. Hearing voices isn't a sign of "madness".* Although words like "madness" and "schizophrenia" can quickly come to people's minds, hearing voices is not uncommon during childhood and can actually be a very helpful way for young people to manage times of distress.

2. *Seek advice sooner rather than later.* Help comes in many forms and it is important that things don't get to a point where young people and parents feel overwhelmed. There are several online communities and sources of direct support that help normalize these experiences and offer reassurance. (See for example http://www.voicecollective.co.uk/support/parents-carers/.)
3. *Show them constant love and support.* The findings of our research and that of colleagues in the field suggest that openness, curiosity, and acceptance can be very helpful responses in dealing with young people. However, if a young voice hearer is met with disbelief or panic, they can feel increasingly distressed and are more likely to experience further difficulties.
4. *Take a day at a time.* Experiences of hearing voices during childhood is rarely a sign of long-term mental health difficulties. Calmness and patience seem to be helpful platforms from which a young person can build upon to find other helpful coping strategies and manage difficulties over time. (See http://www.intervoiceonline.org/3393/news/free-booklets-for-parents.html.)
5. *Keep calm and research it a little bit yourself.* We have had several responses and emails over recent weeks from parents and young people expressing their relief and gratitude that a more compassionate perspective is being taken towards voice hearing. There are many helpful sources of support for young people and families that do not prescribe to the traditional and outdated preconceptions around voice hearing. (See for example https://www.youtube.com/watch?v=VRqI4lxuXAw.)
6. *Try and get health professionals to talk to you.* Some parents have reported that healthcare professionals seemed reluctant or uncomfortable talking about voice hearing. Similarly, our colleagues have also been told by mental health practitioners that they do not feel as though they have sufficient training in relation to these experiences. As such, parents may need to seek out professionals who do have relevant expertise, including experts-by-experience, and make use of helpful advice online through organizations such as the Voice Collective and Hearing Voices Network (at https://www.hearing-voices.org/).

7. *Only be concerned when it is impacting on their sense of wellbeing.* A few of the parents who have responded to our online survey discussed how their older children have heard voices for some time. Generally, the voices seem to have become a manageable part of day-to-day life and often a source of comfort and support for the young person. A couple of parents explained how the voices their child hears are an essential part of how they maintain their positive wellbeing.
8. *We can all be a little "mad" at times, but as long as we understand ourselves and have a range of positive coping strategies, then we do not need to see that difference as negative.* A key message that has come through time and again is that difference is not a bad thing, and neither are the voices. Many of the parents who have been in touch explain that they were nervous at first, not knowing how to talk about their children's experiences; and have then come to see the beneficial impact of the voices as a way their child copes with challenges.
9. *Listen, encourage ongoing dialogue, and support them to normalize the voices.* All of the parents who have kindly offered insights into their experiences have highlighted how essential it is to keep channels of communication open, to keep a curious and open mind, and to hear what the young person needs. This has been seconded by the young people who have also taken part in our study. However, there also seems to be a fine line between "normalizing" and "minimizing"—recognizing the impact of the voices for the young person is also crucial.
10. *Remain calm and reassuring but seek advice and support.* The parents and young people who have shared their experiences have given many examples of trying to find the right support for their particular family circumstances. Parents have explained how isolating it can feel to support a young person who hears voices, until helpful support that meets their needs is found. When parents feel supported, they can increasingly meet the needs of their child, which is why it is so important we involve parents and families in work such as this.

Millions upon millions of words have been written about what constitutes good parenting and how parents can improve their skills. Your job as a helper is not to be expert in every facet of this conversation—no one could be—but rather to serve your parent-clients as a compassionate, caring, and, yes, probing partner as each one tries to deal with his or her distressed, difficult, or diagnosed child. You are there to say "A diagnosis is not the end of the matter" and "Let's see if together we can figure out what might help"—and it is a blessing that you are there to provide that service.

12

THIRTY-ONE QUESTIONS FOR PARENTS

The following 31 questions are provided in case you would like to arm your clients with a set of questions to ponder. Pondering them yourself is also a good idea, as they can help you organize your thinking about the challenges that your clients who are also parents are quite likely facing.

1 What's Going on?

You're a parent. But you're also many other things and you're living a complicated life. You have your own challenges, your own worries, your own past with its disturbances and difficulties, your own dreams and desires, your own intense reality. We hardly know what's going on in our own life—and it's dismaying how long it can take us to know how to live or what's really going on within us and around us. We may never really fully know. It is in the context of a great deal of "not knowing" that we are obliged to approach our parenting and our child. It would be lovely if we knew more, understood better, and could pinpoint the causes of our own sadness or anxiety—or our child's. But can we?

All we can do is acknowledge the bewildering nature of life, appreciate the extent to which presumed experts do not know enough either, and come at life—our own and the lives of those around us, including our children—with compassion, curiosity, and considered attention. Do not rush to some simple answer—for instance, that your child has a so-called mental disorder—when you know that life is more complicated, nuanced, and mysterious than that. Yes, it would be lovely if we understood what's going on. Unfortunately, we are stuck looking at life through a glass darkly. What's really going on, with you, your child, or anyone? Just breathe and consider.

2 Is There a Problem?

Let's say that your child is exhibiting some sort of behavior, like restlessness, or having certain thoughts or feelings, like feelings of sadness. First of all, is it a problem? Is it a problem if, say, your child waits two months longer to speak than did Jane across the street? Why is that a problem as opposed to a natural difference? Is it a problem that he enthusiastically signs up for violin lessons and then wants to stop them after two weeks? Why is that a problem as opposed to a change of heart? Is it a problem that he doesn't want to sit still at the dinner table where you and your mate are fighting? Why is that a problem as opposed to good common sense?

You can label any of these a problem—a developmental delay, a lack of discipline, a refusal to obey—but where is the love, charity, or logic in that? Be careful not to leap to the idea that something your child is doing, thinking, or feeling is a problem, even if it is something that scares you, for instance that he or she is hearing voices. We are being trained to look at just about everything as problematic, so that we can be sold chemical solutions and other "expert" solutions to that problem. There are huge industries out there needing us to call things problems. Take some time and do some investigating before you use the "P" word on something your child is exhibiting.

3 Has My Child Always Been Like This?

If your child has always been shy, why is it suddenly surprising that he or she is still shy now? If your child has always been bursting with energy and bouncing off the walls, why is it suddenly surprising that he or she is still full of energy and still bouncing off the walls? If your child has always been the quiet, brooding one, why is it suddenly surprising that he or she is still quiet and brooding? These may be features of your child's natural endowment or original personality. Or these may be features of his or her formed personality acquired so early on that they have pretty much always been there now. Either way, there is no reason to treat your child's unique ways of being as suddenly surprising.

His or her ways of being may create difficulties, for him or for her or for others, and those difficulties certainly must be addressed. But that isn't to say that your child suddenly "came down" with shyness, restlessness, or brooding tendencies or that those qualities or behaviors are somehow markers of a "mental disorder." Psychology, for all its millions of journal articles, has never studied original personality and has almost nothing to say about how we come into the world already somebody. Yet that is our baseline, our uniqueness, and our reality. Wasn't your child perplexedly and exactly himself or herself from birth? Remember that.

4 Am I Being Pressured into Seeing Problems?

What if the instruments of society—your child's pediatrician, your child's teacher, your child's principal, your child's guidance counselor, etc.—suggest, imply, or announce that your child has a mental disorder? What if you are informed that he or she ought to be treated as soon as possible with a regimen of chemicals; and that to do otherwise is irresponsible on your part, endangers your child's future in school and in life, and is tantamount to child neglect? How can you be expected to think clearly about what's going on, feel as if you have permission to research alternatives, or not succumb to that enormous pressure? When the deck is stacked against you and your child in such powerful ways, how can you successfully resist or calmly proceed?

Step one is to recognize that you *are* being pressured. If someone in a position of power or a supposed expert provides you with exactly one explanation of what is going on—the mental disorder explanation—and you *know* that there must be multiple ways to conceptualize what's going on, you should appreciate that their "one explanation" amounts to implicit pressure on you to believe a certain thing, to react in a certain way, and to grant the powers that be a certain permission. You are having the experience of being pressured because you *are* being pressured. Internally nod and say, "What I'm feeling is real. They are pressuring me!"

5 How Might the Problem Be Conceptualized?

Maybe your child looks to be in distress, maybe he or she is causing disturbances, maybe he or she is very sad or anxious. How should this reality be conceptualized?

Let's paint the following too-simple but useful picture. There are seven ways to look at what's going on. The first is that nothing dramatic is going on and that there is no problem at all. The second is that this is a momentary aberration or transitional phase. The third is that something is "broken" in a medical or biological sense, the underlying premise of the mental disorder paradigm. The fourth is that it's a matter of circumstance, say that he or she is being bullied in school. The fifth is that it's a matter of original personality, like being born with lots of energy, which is now translating itself into restlessness and fidgeting. The sixth is that it's a matter of formed personality, like becoming less confident over time because of school failures. The seventh is that it's a result of family dynamics, like living with an abusive parent.

To repeat, this is a too-simple picture. But it's a useful one, in part because it's a reminder that you *may* be causing or contributing to your child's distress. Therefore, you will need to deal with your natural defensiveness as you try to conceptualize what's going on with your child. Likewise, it's a reminder that the "broken" point of view—the mental disorder paradigm—is not the only way to think about what's going on, and many would say rarely the best way. Please consider this: Surely there is more than one way to conceptualize what's going on with your child, wouldn't you say?

6 How Serious Is the Problem?

Some problems are mountains and some problems are molehills and most problems are somewhere in between. That your two-year-old grabs toys from other children isn't a catastrophic problem. That your adolescent is relying on heroin is another matter entirely. That your child's grades aren't stellar isn't a catastrophic problem, even though it may feel that way as you think about his or her future. That he or she is seriously self-harming is another matter entirely. You do not want to hold all problems as of equal moment and of equal weight.

In the addiction recovery field, for example, there are somewhat clear and fairly useful distinctions made among experimentation, regular use, habitual use, abuse, dependence, and so on. Most of life's challenges, however, don't present themselves in such neat categories. Is your child moody (like almost any adolescent), gloomy, despondent, despairing, or in some even darker place? Under only moderate stress to perform well, under a good deal of stress, or under great stress? Equipped with a rich fantasy life or dangerously lost in fantasy? Happy in solitude or far too isolated? As hard as it is to make fine distinctions when it comes to challenges of this sort, it is still wise to speculate about the mildness or seriousness of a given problem. Often, we do not need to go on high alert; and sometimes we must.

7 What Is My Experience of My Child?

You know your child. Was he or she pretty happy until the divorce, and have things changed dramatically since then? Did he or she give you sly looks even at one year of age—was he or she an impish trickster even then? Was there some part of your child's brain that just hated things being out of order, such that he or she had a tantrum—even a full-fledged meltdown—if something happened out of sequence? Did your child startle easily from birth? Did your child always sleep erratically? Did your child go through periods of eating everything and then eating next to nothing? You know a lot about this odd, wonderful, wild creature, don't you?

Couldn't you have predicted that the way your two-year-old stepped boldly and recklessly off into space on playground structures might turn into bold, reckless, and impulsive adolescent behaviors? Didn't you sense that your child would always be socially anxious and a bit of a loner? If a supposed expert now wants to bundle together certain of your child's behaviors and ways of being and call that bundle a mental disorder, a mental illness, or a mental disease, don't you know better than to quickly nod and agree? If the claim that a supposed expert makes is at odds with what you know to be true about your child, be careful about overriding your intuition and replacing it with someone else's too-quick opinion.

8 What Do I Want for My Child?

In the moment—right now—what you may want is that your child stops bouncing off the walls, throwing tantrums, hating school, playing so many video games, not listening, or acting so morose. Maybe you want him or her to be less curt, less weird, more helpful, less sullen, less defiant, a better student, more responsible, or less annoying. All of that is what you want from your child. But what do you want for your child? That turns out to be a very hard question to answer because it involves us in significant contradictions. Do we want what we want or what our child wants? And even if our wants are congruent, how do we help our child get there?

We want our child to be happy but we also know that our child is bound to have to deal with many unhappy events and circumstances—unpleasant jobs, career disappointments, relationship breakups, illnesses, and all the rest. Do we steel our child to that reality? Or do we gloss that over? Do we try to produce a little Stoic or a little Pollyanna? Do we encourage our child to be the dancer he or she wants to be or almost anything else? Do we try to encourage our child to be more sociable, for his or her own sake, even though he or she is dreadfully shy? Or do we hope that with time he or she will outgrow that social anxiety? What outcomes do we want? And is pressing for them the right game plan?

Embrace how difficult it is to answer the question, "What do I want for my child?" The mental disorder paradigm makes it seem as if all that we are after as parents is the elimination of our child's "symptoms." Is that all that we want for our child? Is that even the main thing? Or is the picture more complicated than that?

9 Have There Been Any Big (or Small) Changes Recently?

If your child's circumstances change, he or she is likely to react to those changes. Is your child in a new school? Doing new, harder schoolwork? Dealing with your separation or divorce? Living in a new town? Dealing with a new sibling? Did he or she move from a single room to a shared room? Have there been any changes in his or her diet or exercise? Was there more junk food intake than usual or less exercise during a long winter? Changes in circumstances matter. It makes sense to think through whether any changes in your child's circumstances or your family's circumstances might be contributing to your child's current distress or difficulties.

Your child's natural development brings with it changes, too. Do you expect your toddler not to want to hold the spoon himself or herself at some point? Is that a completely unexpected battle? Do you expect your sweet child not to grow rebellious when adolescence hits? Do you expect your child not to be affected by the documentary he or she just watched that suddenly causes him or her to become a vegetarian, a pacifist, a Buddhist, or an artist? Your child is organizing and reorganizing his or her inner world and that constant inner constructing amounts to real and sometimes significant change. Should you construe that new attitude or behavior as a "symptom" or as a change? Why the former and not the latter?

Your child's circumstances may have changed and your child's inner reality may have changed. Mustn't all that be factored in as you try to figure out what's going on?

10 Is My Child under Stress?

You might not think that your child having a prominent part in the school play might prove a source of serious stress for him or her. But it might. The same might hold true for an upcoming piano recital, spelling bee, public event, or competition. Is your child taking a harder math class than last year or a history or language class that requires massive memorization? Challenges of this sort and many of the other challenges of childhood and the school years produce real, significant stress. And that stress is likely to play itself out as distress and difficulty.

Take time to consider the link between stress and distress in your child's life. Childhood, adolescence, and young adulthood are anything but stress free. To be holding some romantic or idyllic notion of the ease of childhood flies in the face of reality. You know how stressed out your child can get: will he or she be invited to that A-list birthday party, are pimples appearing again, did someone call him or her fat? Isn't it possible that stress, and not a putative "mental disorder," is causing your child's sleep problems, bed-wetting, tantrums, irritability, forgetfulness, underperformance, sadness, or other so-called "symptom"? Doesn't that seem logical and even likely?

11 Is My Family under Stress?

Kids can feel family stress in their bones. Your young child may not know that you and your mate are struggling to pay the bills or regularly at each other's throat but he or she is very well aware that *something* is going on. Your child picks up on cold silences, sarcastic remarks, and stress in the air. Even infants react to the stress around them. That's why family therapists assume that a child's problems are related to family dynamics. Of course, family dynamics may not be contributing to your child's difficulties—but they may. If they are, isn't that a very different lens through which to view your child's troubles than the "mental disorder" lens?

You know if your family is under stress. But it may prove hard to frankly admit it, maybe because it feels embarrassing not to be living a picture-perfect life, maybe because you can't see any way out of your situation, or for some other reason. Even if it's hard to do so, acknowledge that stress, for the sake of your child, yourself, and your whole family. And then what, after you've acknowledged it? Do what you can to reduce it. You can't control life, you can't control others, you can't make big changes with a snap of your fingers. But maybe there are some things to try, even some quite simple things, that will make a positive difference. Isn't that a possibility worth thinking about?

12 Has My Child Been Abused or Traumatized?

Trauma and abuse produce distress. Sometimes called "adverse childhood experiences," even a single traumatic event, incident of abuse, or adverse childhood experience can cause difficulties in the moment and lifetime negative consequences. If the trauma persists, that makes matters worse; and if there are multiple adverse childhood experiences, like neglect piled on abuse or several bullies in the family, that also makes matters worse. The trauma, abuse, or adverse childhood experience can occur in the home, at school, or affect whole communities, say when floods or earthquakes strike. And they can occur out of the clear blue sky, say if your child suddenly comes into close contact with a predatory priest, gymnastics coach, or other unidentified felon.

If your child comes home from summer camp and seems not to be his or her usual self, doesn't it make sense to check in with him or her to see if something abusive or traumatic occurred at camp? Has there been a death in the family, the death of one of your child's friends, or the death of a pet? Is your family life so chaotic as to rise to the level of the traumatic? Has someone like a difficult aging parent recently moved into the home? Looking at matters from your child's perspective, might there be issues of abuse or trauma that he or she is trying to deal with (and maybe keeping secret about)? These are not pleasant matters to think about, especially if a family member is the culprit. But protecting your child from trauma and abuse is your duty.

13 Is There Someone Mean in My Child's Life?

Researchers estimate that as much as a quarter of the population is authoritarian: bullying, controlling, punishing, and just plain mean. The likelihood is high that your child will come into contact with mean people—in your own home, at school, at church, among his friends, at after-school activities, at band practice or soccer practice: somewhere. Even occasional contact with mean people can prove damaging. But prolonged contact is inevitably harmful. Is it possible that what's troubling your child is connected to past contact with a mean person or the ongoing presence of a mean person in his or her life?

In my primary research with victims of authoritarian wounding, I've learned that sometimes the mean person is a grandparent, an aunt or uncle, or a sibling; and that even limited contact with that mean person —say, the occasional holiday event with that bullying uncle—can prove wounding. Does your child seem particularly anxious before one of these events or sadder or more troubled than usual after it? Doesn't that provide you with important clues about what might be causing your child's troubles? Mean people, aggressive people, bullying people: they do harm. Presume that if such a person is in your child's life that contact is negatively affecting your child and may amount to a complete explanation of your child's difficulties.

14 Who Has the Problem?

If your mate belittles your child and your child grows sad and withdrawn, your child certainly has a problem. But isn't your mate the real problem? If you are highly anxious and vigilant and your child becomes highly anxious and vigilant, your child certainly has a problem. But what's your part in the equation? If yours is a rigid and dogmatic household and your child rebels against your house rules, your child certainly has a problem. But isn't the family's rigidity its own sort of problem? I'm not raising this matter to assign blame or to make anyone feel guilty. Rather it's a matter of appraising the situation honestly so that genuine answers can be found.

If your child is angry, isn't it logical to ask, "Why is he angry?" rather than to announce "He has an anger problem!" If your child is despondent, isn't it logical to ask, "Why is she so sad?" rather than to presume that she is something called "clinically depressed"? Your child may have no answers and indeed you may not have a great deal of luck getting at the why of the matter. But aren't the twin questions "What might be causing this?" and "Who really has the problem?" good starting points? You may be seeing the effect of some cause that, if identified, could be dealt with better. That's a possibility worth exploring,

15 If Someone Else Has the Problem, What Will I Do?

Let's say that you come to recognize that your child's acting out has to do with the fact that you and your mate are obliged to move every few years for work. That obligatory move is putting a strain on your child, who must continually deal with being an outsider at a new school. There may be no perfect answer to this dilemma but there are surely things to try. You might ask your child, "What would make our moving easier on you?" You might take your child on ahead, before the move, and see if you can get him a little bit enthusiastic about his new surroundings. You might invite his input into where you'll live, grant him a special wish as part of the move, or help him figure out how to stay in touch with the friends he's leaving. These efforts just might help.

What if the problem is someone mean in the family—say, your mate? Many millions of couples sweep issues like a cruel parent under the rug and act like nothing is wrong—until, as often happens, one mate finally leaves the other. But you don't want to do that, do you? I'm sure that you don't want your child treated cruelly year in and year out. The very least efforts you might make are to admit what's going on, call your mate on his or her cruelty, and better shield your child from that cruelty. If the problems your child is having are being caused by someone in the family, that is a clarion call to action. You may hate confrontations; taking action may scare you; you may not be very practiced at speaking up. But your child is counting on you. If you won't protect him or her, who will?

16 What Does My Child Say?

Have you asked your child what's going on? Asking is very different from accusing or interrogating. Have you had a quiet, compassionate, heart-to-heart conversation with your child in which you express your worries, announce your love, listen to your child's concerns, and collaborate with him or her on creating some strategies that might help your child deal with the problems that he or she is experiencing? Are you in the habit of checking in with your child so as to understand what he or she is thinking and feeling? If you haven't gotten into that habit, wouldn't that be a great habit to cultivate?

Of course, your child may be close-lipped, have no way to express what's going on, feel scared about pointing a finger, feel obliged to act like everything's okay, and in other ways prove uncommunicative or evasive. This will test your patience; therefore, you will need to be your most patient. Set up such chats so that you are undisturbed, maybe by making an outing of it or waiting until the younger kids are asleep. Even if a given chat goes nowhere, you are announcing that you are available for such chats and that your child can feel safe revealing what's bothering him or her. Wouldn't it seem rather odd to ask everyone under the sun what's going on with your child and not ask your child? Ask him or her first.

17 What Do Other People Say?

Have you checked in with the people in your circle and your community: your mate, your other children, your parents, and anyone else who knows your child well? What are their thoughts about what's going on? They may have nothing useful or productive to offer or they may have some very important insights into what's happening. Ask the people who know your child what they think might be going on. Make a special effort to check in with those people who seem the most level-headed and whose opinions you respect the most. Is there a friend you always turn to when you're having problems? Maybe that's also the right person to chat with about your child's difficulties.

As you chat with the people in your circle, see how they come at challenges and how they conceptualize what helps. Is one quick to suggest specialists? Is another quite skeptical of the supposed expertise of mental health practitioners? Does a third have first-hand experience of what goes on in a mental health treatment facility or first-hand experience with psychiatric medication? Some of these topics may prove sensitive, so by all means tread carefully. But do courageously tread. You don't want to miss learning exactly what you need to know because you feel embarrassed about broaching what feels like an awkward subject. Even if you don't land on pertinent advice, you may discover that some inner wisdom has gotten activated, providing you with a better sense of what you want to try next.

18 Is My Child's Behavior Genuinely Worrisome?

Who hasn't watched a young child obsessively build a tall structure out of blocks, knock it down, build it up again, knock it down again, and keep doing that for a long half hour? What is going on there? Is the child gaining mastery of something? Does it somehow just feel good? Are both creating and destroying necessary activities in a child's life? Surely there is no need to pathologize that half hour! We must be careful not to start down the road of labeling just because our child is doing something that by our standards seems like "too much" or "a little odd." You could label that half hour "symptomatic of obsessive-compulsive behavior" or you could say that it is just what childhood looks like—and wouldn't the latter be truer?

What is normal and what is abnormal? Are those medical terms, statistical terms, or social terms? Is what one culture calls normal also normal in all other cultures? If your child eats dirt, is that a "symptom of a mental disorder" or a craving for minerals lacking in his or her diet? If your young son loves dresses, is that weird or an expression of his basic orientation? Is even something as seemingly out of the ordinary as hearing voices that unusual or worrisome? New research speculates that it may be quite common and only worrisome depending on what the voices are saying. If our child breaks an arm, we have no doubt that something needing attention has happened. But which feelings, moods, attitudes, and behaviors require similar attention? Don't you agree that defining "normal" can't really be such an easy matter?

19 Do I Feel Kindly toward My Child?

Human beings do not automatically love other human beings. Nor is love a stable, impregnable sort of thing. You may have lost patience with your child, feel oppressed by him or her, or in some other way lost that loving feeling. Do you soften in his or her presence and want to hug your child or do you harden in his or her presence and routinely do some scolding? What child wouldn't grow sadder or angrier if he or she felt that what came from a parent wasn't love but criticism or even revulsion? Think whether a softening and a more loving attitude might amount to great medicine.

An excellent social psychology experiment had seminary students rushing to hear a lecture about the Good Samaritan—rushing so fast that they couldn't be bothered to stop to help a person in need. Virtually no seminary student could act like a Good Samaritan because he was in a rush to hear a lecture on the Good Samaritan! Either a person walks the talk or he or she doesn't. Show your child love, feel loving toward your child, come from a place of kindness, consideration, and compassion, and see if your child doesn't listen better, cooperate more, look less sad, throw fewer tantrums, or otherwise improve. And you might feel better yourself, both because your child is having an easier time of it and because those revitalized loving feelings circulating through your system are warming you and cheering you.

20 Am I Quick to Accept Labels for Myself?

How do you describe your own difficulties to yourself and to others? Do you say things like, "Oh, I have ADD and our little Bobby has it too"? Or "Depression runs in our family"? Or "We can't seem to get Sally's anxiety meds right—but I have the same problem myself"? If this is the way that you conceptualize your difficulties and the difficulties of others, aren't you likely to nod in agreement if and when a professional were to assert that your child had a mental disorder? Wouldn't you be inclined to nod whether or not there was any medical evidence or other evidence that your child really did have such a condition? Wouldn't that amount to a pretty automatic nod?

Educate yourself about alternate visions that reject the idea that because you have a certain experience, say of anxiety, you have a "mental disorder" and must take "medication" for that so-called mental disorder. Be a little less quick to accept such labels for yourself or for your children and do some diligent research in this area. It is easy to be seduced by the power of analogy into believing that a "mental disorder" is something like a "physical disorder," just because they sound sort of the same. Investigate the matter and decide for yourself whether you believe that they are even slightly similar. Is "oppositional defiant disorder," for example, anything at all like "cancer"? Be a little less quick to accept mental disorder labeling, either for yourself, a loved one, or your child.

21 Has My Child Had a Full Medical Workup Recently?

What if your child's school difficulties have to do with poor eyesight or poor hearing? What if his or her lethargy, pain complaints, or sleeplessness are symptoms of a medical condition? See if you can rule out genuine organic and biological causes for the "symptoms" that your child is displaying before supposing that they are "symptoms" of a "mental disorder."

Unfortunately, the root causes of human behaviors are not so easily traced back to medical conditions even when such conditions exist. Equally unfortunately, the medical profession is under constant pressure from the pharmaceutical industry to shrink the normal range and increase the abnormal range of everything, paving the way for the prescription of chemicals. So, it may prove hard for doctors to accurately diagnosis a medical condition that actually exists and hard for them to restrain themselves from diagnosing conditions that do not truly exist.

Still, as possibly frustrating as the experience may prove, make sure that a medical workup is part of your plan to help your child with his or her current difficulties. And if that visit culminates in the doctor wanting to diagnose your child with a mental disorder, make sure to ask the following question: "In the absence of hard science that suggests that feelings, attitudes, and behaviors are medical problems, why are you treating this like a medical problem?" See if the answer you get satisfies you—or if you get any answer at all. A medical workup is a necessity, in case a genuine medical condition is present. But be alert to the ways in which such a visit can lead to a spurious, non-medical, mental disorder diagnosis.

22 What Sort of Help Am I Looking For?

You may decide that you can't do enough to help your child reduce his or her experience of distress all by yourself. Where should you turn for help? It amounts to a very different decision to take your child to a child psychologist whose specialty is talk and who uses techniques like play therapy or to take your child to a psychiatrist who routinely "diagnoses mental disorders" and who then "prescribes medication." There are many types of helpers out there—peer counselor, school counselor, mentor, dietician, family therapist, residential treatment specialist, clinical psychologist, psychotherapist, psychiatrist—and each comes at human challenges from a different angle. Educate yourself as to what these different service providers actually provide and decide which sort of service makes the most sense to you.

Let's say that your teenager is getting poor grades, doesn't have friends, is morose, describes life as meaningless, and experiences great social anxiety. Will you aim for help for one of these, say by searching out a tutor to help with his math difficulties or a psychotherapist for his social anxiety? Will you presume that these are all connected under the banner of "difficult teenage years" and press for peer counseling or a coping skills workshop? Or will you go down the road of psychiatry, which will lead to a mental disorder diagnosis and chemicals? How you (and your child) conceptualize "What's going on?" and "What might help?" will send you in one direction or another. Stay steady that the two questions "What's going on?" and "What might help?" matter, even as you feel pulled to throw up your hands and aim your child at the first putative helper that pops to mind. Seriously considering these questions, even if you can't land on perfect answers, will remind you that you have choices, that one choice might prove better than another choice, and that when you decide to try out one sort of help that doesn't preclude you from also trying out some other sort of help.

23 What Do I Make of the Expertise of Experts?

So-called mental disorders are not "diagnosed" based on causes that can be tested for (or even articulated) but are instead "diagnosed" according to what are called symptom pictures. This is a highly questionable practice. For example, what is the logic in calling defiance a "symptom of the mental disorder of oppositional defiant disorder"? Why isn't it just defiance? Why is questioning rules a "symptom of the mental disorder of oppositional defiant disorder"? Why isn't it just questioning rules? Why is "excessive arguing with adults" a "symptom of the mental disorder of oppositional defiant disorder"? Why isn't it just arguing a lot (and maybe for good reason)? What justifies the leap from defiance, questioning rules, and arguing with adults to the pseudo-medical sounding mental disorder label "oppositional defiant disorder," given that there is zero rationale for doing so?

You may be thinking,

> Well, maybe the system is flawed, but surely psychiatrists, psychologists, family therapists, and other mental health professionals

know what to *do* with these symptom pictures. Maybe it isn't exactly science but maybe it is an art, where, through practice, mental health professionals begin to discern the difference between a mental disorder and a life challenge. So, even though the system is flawed, no doubt practitioners *do* know important things about mental disorders.

You would be mistaken in that belief and that puts you in a very difficult position. If you can't really trust the basic premises of psychiatry, what are you supposed to do? No one has perfect or even very good answers. But at least there are many things that you might try, from educating yourself about the pros and cons of so-called psychiatric medication to improving your parenting skills and reducing family stress to exploring alternative resources like peer counseling, mentoring, play therapy, and talk therapy. It is very hard on you that you can't really trust mental health providers to know what they are doing, to have a solid rationale for what they are doing, or to be making claims based on solid science. Still you must persevere, even if no one you encounter is really the expert he or she claims to be.

24 Who Has a Vested Interest in My Child's Disorder?

The profit motive is a powerful motive in human affairs. Pharmaceutical companies make huge profits by supplying powerful chemicals called psychiatric medications that are touted as safely and effectively treating things called mental disorders. If you are merely in despair, they have no way to make a profit from you. If that despair is given the medical-sounding name clinical depression, then they can provide a medical-seeming pill called an antidepressant. These medical-seeming pills may indeed have an effect on you, either a placebo effect, some other positive effect, or a negative effect. Pharmaceutical companies have a large and natural vested interest in selling these chemicals, as they are profitable and because the model—that mental disorders can be created by professionals sitting around a table—assures mental disorder growth and future sales.

However, pharmaceutical companies aren't the only ones with a vested interest in the mental disorder paradigm. Universities and university researchers need it, because it is an avenue to research dollars. Mental health professionals need it, because it bolsters their prestige, makes them look like experts, and provides a rationale for what they do. The courts need it, as a way to provide some distinctions between who is in their right mind and who isn't. Society needs it, as a mechanism for controlling unruly and unwanted public behaviors. Schools need it, for the same reasons. This web of need extends far and wide and includes more folks than you might suppose. It even includes your friends, neighbors, and loved ones, who have their own vested interest in believing in a model that looks and smells like medicine. Most people are invested in their culture's dominant paradigms and tend to believe them unquestioningly. So, who has a vested interest in your child's mental disorder? Just about everyone.

25 What Is the Rationale for Labeling My Child with a Mental Disorder?

If a mental health professional would like to give your child a mental disorder label, for instance the label ADHD, inquire as to his or her rationale for doing so. Ask questions like, "By 'mental disorder' do you mean 'medical issue'?" "If you do not mean 'medical issue,' why do you want to prescribe medicine for my child?" "If you do mean 'medical issue,' please explain to me what the medical issue is and what the evidence for it is." There are many more questions you might want to ask so as to satisfy yourself that the idea of "diagnosing and treating mental disorders" makes sense to you. Will your child's provider be willing or able to answer your questions? See for yourself. Will the provider's answers, if you get any, make sense to you or satisfy you? See for yourself.

Imagine asking your surgeon, "Why are planning to cut me open?" and getting no answer. Or getting the answer, "Because it's a surgical issue." Or getting the answer, "Because you have a bio-psycho-social problem." Or getting the answer, "It's a statistical matter." Or getting the answer, "Because of your symptom picture." This one might impress you and you will need to educate yourself regarding the huge holes in the "symptom picture" method of "diagnosing mental disorders." Or getting the answer, "Because of an abnormality." This one might also impress you until you dig a little bit into what "normal" and "abnormal" seem to mean to mental health practitioners. Since the leap made by mental health professionals from observed behavior to a mental disorder diagnosis is a labeling leap and not a medical leap or a scientific leap, the answers they provide will likely cause you to shake your head. Make sure that the rationale for this whole business makes sense to you.

26 What Is the Rationale for Prescribing My Child Powerful Chemicals?

Human beings have always taken substances because of their effects. We are very accustomed to this idea. What we are not accustomed to doing is taking a close look at why we are taking a given substance. What heavy drinker wants to take a close look at his or her rum or vodka intake? What insomniac doesn't prefer popping a sleeping pill to engaging in the hard work of reducing his or her stress? Weight watchers want their amphetamines, men suffering from performance anxiety or limited interest grab their Viagra, women will inject the neurotoxin Botox to remove wrinkles. Since that is where we are, very comfortable taking chemicals for any and every reason and loathe to scrutinize that intake, it follows that the average parent is primed to accept the idea that his or her child's diagnosis should naturally lead to a chemical fix.

Even if you assume that the psychiatric chemicals given to children work, which is a highly debatable assumption, that they work is not the only criteria by which to judge whether or not a chemical should be taken. Vast amounts of Scotch may work to help you forget that you hate your life but that doesn't make alcoholism an excellent treatment for despair. When it comes to the psychiatric chemicals that may be prescribed to your child, as important to answer as "Do they work?" are "Do they make sense?" and "Are they a good idea?" First of all, how often and to what extent do they work (remembering that there is no scientific evidence to support the idea that a medical condition is present)? Second, do they make sense at all, if mental disorders are labels and not medical conditions? Third, are they are a good idea, given their powerful side effects, the possibility that alternatives may be available, and vexing questions of dependence, addiction, and more? Make sure to answer these three questions to your own satisfaction.

27 What Other Avenues Might I Try?

Let's say that your child is despondent. You might send your child down the road of mental disorder labeling and chemicals. But surely there are other things you might also try, either instead of the label-and-chemical route or simultaneous with that route. You might investigate whether that despondency has something to do with diet and nutrients. You might wonder if it has something to do with family dynamics—for instance, that your mate bullies your child—and make an effort to improve the situation. You might wonder if it has something to do with an event that's just transpired or is about to happen—say, the death of a pet or a pet's impending euthanasia—and treat the situation as one of grief, educating yourself about what helps someone who is grieving. The list is very long as to how you might conceptualize the situation and what avenues you might try.

How can you know what's making your child despondent before you do a little investigating? Do you feel sanguine that turning your child over to a mental health professional who only knows to go down the first route is everything that you can or should do? Doesn't it make good sense to try to arrive at thoughtful answers to the 31 questions I'm posing in this chapter? It is holding the bar too high to suppose that you will become some sort of expert in these matters, since frankly no one is. But I know that you agree that exploring additional avenues makes sense. The first steps might be making a nice, long list of the possible causes of whatever is ailing your child and then identifying something to try for each possible cause. Doesn't that sound like important parental homework?

28 Is My Child Actually Getting Any Better?

If you've tried to help your child in some way, whether via a traditional psychiatric intervention or via something else, the next question to address is whether your child is getting better, whether the situation remains unchanged, or whether your child's situation has worsened. It seems as if this should be easy to gauge but in fact it isn't really that easy. Multiple studies have shown that if a child is being prescribed psychiatric medication, both parents and teachers will report that the child is doing much better, even if there's no observable change. Perception gets significantly mixed with reality when it comes to judging whether or not our child is faring better. And is "doing better" all that ought to concern you, given that the long-term negative effects of psychiatric chemicals may not appear immediately? Is your child doing better in the moment at the cost of doing more poorly down the road? And what does "better" even mean, for instance when it comes to sedating an active child?

Say that your child is placed on so-called psychiatric medication and his or her situation worsens. You will then be faced with the following very difficult questions. Is your child's condition actually worsening and is the so-called medication proving ineffective (and therefore perhaps ought to be changed or increased, which is likely what your child's psychiatrist will recommend)? Or is it the case that the so-called medication is actually causing the worsening (there is ample evidence that this can happen)? If your child's situation doesn't improve you are caught in the predicament of trying to figure out what's going on with your child while also needing to appraise the effectiveness or dangerousness of the help being offered your child.

29 If My Child Is Getting Worse, What Will I Do?

Let's say that your child has been extremely sad, has been diagnosed with a so-called mental disorder and put on so-called psychiatric medication, and is now quite worse, deeper in despair, and talking about suicide more often. How should you think about this moment? Your child's mental health provider is likely to promote the idea that your child either needs a different dose of the antidepressant he or she is taking, a different antidepressant, or an additional antidepressant. What he or she is unlikely to suggest is that your child's worsening is a direct result of taking these particular powerful chemicals, many of which are known to increase despair and thoughts of suicide. Given that your child's helper is unlikely to provide this information, you would naturally feel pressured to go along with his or her suggestion regarding a change in meds. But now that you know that the chemicals themselves might be causing the deterioration, what should you do?

No one knows for sure. How can you know for sure when it isn't clear whether, in a particular case, taking a chemical helps the best or not taking that chemical will help more or whether something additional or different ought to be tried? At the very least, you would want to try the following. You would want to put this conundrum on the table in your conversations with your child's helper and not act like you are sanguine about the chemical fix route. You would want to see to what extent more talk can help, either with you, a talk therapist, or with someone with whom your child talks most easily. You would want to research other options and see if you come to some intuitive understanding that maybe what's wanted is a therapeutic wilderness experience, a mentor, a change in diet, less stress put on your child, a less isolating life for your child, or some other alternative. In this difficult situation, with only imperfect solutions, these three are the least that you ought to try: a fuller conversation about the chemicals that your child may be taking, efforts at more talk with your child, and a wide-ranging investigation of alternative approaches to helping and healing.

30 What about Me?

You have your own life, your own needs, and your own challenges. If parenting is demoralizing you or depleting you, you need your own self-care and support. You may be caught in a vortex of difficulty, trying to deal not only with one child but with his or her siblings, with your mate, with your parents—and then there are all of your social and existential needs, your need for friends, meaning, and all the rest. Life lived this way is like a hurricane. It is a fair question and not a selfish question to ask, "What do I need?" Unless you ask that question and arrive at some satisfactory answers, you may be jeopardizing your physical health and your emotional wellbeing and coming to the table of life as a weakened version of yourself.

Do you need to ask someone to help for the day? Ask. Do you need to completely rethink how you are holding career and home life? Do that rethinking. Do you need to institute a healing practice for the mind or for the body? Start that. Do you need to heal from early trauma? Learn how that is possible and try out something you learn. Is your anxiety high? Learn and use some anxiety management strategy, maybe something as simple as a little intentional deep breathing. Are you always hungry, always craving, always rushing? Face your own appetites and your own racing energy. I have been addressing you as a parent but you are a person too. What do you need? What must you do? Consider.

31 What Should I Be Doing?

We've tackled 31 questions. Answering them will help you look at what's going on in your child's life from a much broader perspective, one that takes into account the many pitfalls of the mental disorder paradigm and that includes the significant alternatives available to you. I think that trying to answer these 31 questions is a thing that you ought to do. A given answer may prove eye-opening and some answers may lead you to simple remedies with great positive effects. For instance, you might land on the simply remedy of being easier on your child if he is the youngest in his class and acting more immaturely than his peers. Or the simple remedy of having a conversation with your daughter that quells some of her fears about the impending divorce.

Even if the matter remains opaque, difficult, and disheartening, you are bound to know more than when you began and be at least somewhat better equipped to deal with the situation. You will have trained yourself to wonder if what is going on might be a feature of your child's original personality and therefore a difference rather than a disorder. You'll have become knowledgeable about everything from peer counseling programs to alternative residential models. And you'll be less likely to accept that your child has something called a mental disorder just because a certain catalogue says so. Will you have landed on the perfect solution? Fingers crossed that you will have! But you will certainly have done the smart, loving thing.

**

BIBLIOGRAPHY

American Psychiatric Association. (2013). *Diagnostic and statistical manual of mental disorders* (5th ed.). Arlington, VA: Author.

Johns Hopkins Medicine. (n.d.). Oppositional Defiant Disorder (ODD) in children. Retrieved from www.hopkinsmedicine.org/healthlibrary/conditions/mental_health_disorders/oppositional_defiant_disorder_90, P02573

MacCabe, J.H., Lambe, M.P., Cnattingius, S., Sham, P.C., David, A.S., Reichenberg, A., Murray, R.M., & Hultman, C.M. (2010). Excellent school performance at age 16 and risk of adult bipolar disorder: National cohort study. *The British Journal of Psychiatry*, 196(2), 109–115. doi:10.1192/bjp.bp.108.060368

O'Neil, A., Quirk, S.E., Housden, S., Brennan, S.L., Williams, L.J., Pasco, J.A., Berk, M., & Jacka, F.N. (2014). Relationship between diet and mental health in children and adolescents: A systematic review. *American Journal of Public Health*, 104(10), e31–e42. doi:10.2105/AJPH.2014.302110

WebMD Medical Reference. (2018, May 20). Oppositional Defiant Disorder. Retrieved from www.webmd.com/mental-health/oppositional-defiant-disorder#1

Whitaker, R. (2010). *Anatomy of an epidemic: Magic bullets, psychiatric drugs, and the astonishing rise of mental illness in America.* New York, NY: Crown Publishers.

INDEX

American Psychiatric Association 6–7, 25–26
Artreach, Inc. 122–124
assertive community treatment (ACT) 142–144
Atkins, Rebecca 122–124
attention deficit hyperactivity disorder (ADHD): contextual framing of behavior 34, 35, 40–41, 42–43; description not diagnosis 18, 19; detrimental labeling 35, 37; 'diagnosis' variables 30–31; late birthday effect 36; as linguistic product 41–42; Native Indian children's mislabeling 38–39; neurotoxin exposure 97, 98; placebo effect 79–80; prescription accountability 34–35, 37–38; societal perceptions 39–40; test validity, right to challenge 31–33; treatment, commercial bias 36

Australia: ADHD prevalence 34–35, 36; Rogue & Rouge Foundation 130–132
autism 97, 98

Berezin, Robert 40–41
biological psychiatry 35, 36, 37
bipolar disorder: depression, perceptions and realities 64–69; high intelligence and creativity links 60–61; juvenile bipolar 57–60, 63–64, 70; mania and racing brain 60, 61–62; non-medicated perspective 119–120
Burstow, Bonnie 55–56, 80–81

Carey, Tim 170–173
causes, contributory factors: behavioral matter 90–91; biological misconceptions 89–90; change of circumstance 94, 190,

193–194; cultural and societal 95–96, 195–196; developmental age 88–89; dietary 96–100; emotional upsets 93–94; endowment (aptitude) 92; environmental 96, 97–98; experiences 91–92; family dynamics 90, 191, 193–194; formed personality 87, 186; internal/external lenses 85–86; life purpose and meaning 100–101; mind space and indwelling 88; neurotoxin exposure 97, 98; original personality 87, 186; parental introspection 86; psychiatric medications 100; psychological experiences 94–95; social world 91; stress 92–93, 190–191; trauma 93, 191–193
chemicals, contextual distinctions 73–75
Collaborative & Proactive Solutions (CPS) 52–54
Cook, Jo Ann 75–78
Creating Communities 124–128

depression: 'disease' mislabeling 26; perceptions and realities 64–69
diagnosis: differentiating cause from symptoms 15–17; DSM's influence 21–22, 25–26; illegitimacy and dangers 27–29; medical not psychiatric process 18–21; no-labeling alternatives 156–159; professional debate 24
Diamond, Jed 106–107

Dillon, Jacqui 138–141
Dorfman, Kelly 99
DSM (Diagnostic and Statistical Manual of Mental Disorders): commercial and ethical impact 27; definitions as fraudulent 21–22; diagnoses, validity questioned 6–7, 25–26; ODD definition 48; standardization 25

Elliott, Carl 41–42
epigenetics 98
Extended Therapy Room Foundation 128–130

Families Healing Together 119–122
family therapy 111
Furlong, Mark 141–144

Gibson, Nicole 130–132
Gilbert, Michael 117–119
Gould Farm, therapeutic community 133–135
Greenberg, Gary 24–27
Greene, Ross W. 51–54
Green, Tabita 58–59
group psychotherapy 108–109

Hakansson, Carina 128–130
Healy, Maureen 174–177
hearing voices: organizational resources 138–140, 150; parenting guidance 180–182; personal experiences 148
Hearing Voices Network 138–141, 148, 150

Insel, Thomas 6
It's About Childhood & Family, Inc. 117–119

juvenile bipolar disorder: behavior misinterpreted 57–58, 59–60, 70; 'depression', misuse of label 63–64; medication, negative effects 58–59; see also bipolar disorder

Kuhn, Rosie 113–115

LaCerva, Christine 109–111
language, critical analysis: diagnosis and no-labeling alternatives 156–159; normal/abnormal, concept misuse 152–155
Levit, Rob 124–128
Linsley, Jane 133–135
Longden, Eleanor 147–150
Lucas, Catherine G. 135–138

Mackinnon, Krista 119–122
manic-depression see bipolar disorder
marijuana 74–75
medication: chemical cure myth 78–79, 83, 140–141, 204; chemicals, contextual distinctions 73–75; clinical proposal, challenging questions 81–82, 201–202; crisis stabilization 106, 134–135; 'diagnosis' and medicalization 11, 17, 20, 71–72, 119–120, 200–201; institutional advocacy concerns 75–76; juvenile bipolar, mistreatment of 58–59; ODD subjugation 45–46; placebo effect 79–80, 83; practitioner as information broker 78–79, 120, 151–152; practitioner evaluations 132, 137–138, 143; psychiatric drug risks 72–73, 76–78, 80–81, 100, 204–205; psychiatric drugs over prescription 2–3, 4–5, 37–38, 73, 141; short-term and planned withdrawal 83–84
mental disorders: detrimental labeling 35, 38; DSM definitions as fraudulent 21–22, 26; excessive 'diagnosis' and medication 2–3, 4–5, 20; excessive diagnosis and medication 200–201; labeling, questioning rationale 201–202; as linguistic product 41–42, 153; multifaceted reasons and parental dilemmas 8–12; non-medicated parenting 7–8, 38; pseudo-science critiques 5–7, 12; 'symptom picture' model 5, 35, 45, 63, 199–200; test validity, right to challenge 31–33
Milestones of Recovery Scale (MORS) 145
mindfulness practices 103–104, 137
Moncrieff, Joanna 78–79, 140–141

normal/abnormal, concept misuse 152–155

Olfman, Sharna 6, 97–98
oppositional defiant disorder (ODD): child's assessment,

INDEX

parental guidance 47–50; explosive child, parenting tips 51–54; finding causes 47, 54; mental disorder, suspect evaluations 50–51, 54–56; parent/teacher self-help skills 174–177; subjugation and medication 45–46; symptoms and labeling 45, 47

organizational resources: arts/creative based practices and activities 122–128; community-based services 117–119; education and mentoring 124–128, 131; relational approach 119–122; shared life-skills and practices 128–130; youth empowerment and facilitation 130–132

parental stress 3–4, 13, 186–187, 191
parenting: basic support 38; behavior in context 40–41, 42–43; causes of behavior, contribution to 86, 90, 93, 95–96, 100–101; causes of behavior, positive understanding 87–96; dietary monitoring 96–97, 98–99; environmental stressors, awareness of 96, 97, 98; medicalization of behavior 20, 89–90, 100; ODD assessment, taking control 47–50; ODD self-help guidance 51–54, 174–177; presence, overcoming avoidance tactics 177–179; reflective questions and explanations 170–173; test validity, right to challenge 31–33, 152; well-being challenges 205–206

parents, evaluative and reflective questions: abuse or trauma issues 191–192; change of circumstance 190, 193–194; child centered talks 194–195; child's stress points 190–191; complications of life 184–185; disorder diagnosis, motives for 200–201; distinguishing problems 185–186; emotional connection 196–197; family/friends dynamics 193–194; family under stress 191; friends, learning from 195; labeling pressures 186–187, 189; mean people, contact with 192–193; medical conditions, check for 197–198; mental disorder labeling 201–202; mental health experts 199–200; moving forward 206; non-medical investigations 203; normality and labeling 195–196; parental well-being 205–206; personality traits 188–189; psychiatric medication dilemmas 202–203, 204–205; recovery perceptions 203–204; seeking help 198–199; self labeling 197; seriousness of problem 188; what's wanted for child 189

Parry, Sarah 180–182
peer mentoring and counseling 112
pharmaceutical industry 36, 37, 59, 73, 200
practitioner-parent sessions: abilities and practice

improvement 162; abnormality concept discussed 152–155; coaching vignettes 163–168; critical approach to treatment 12–14, 151–152; hearing and wondering aloud 160; labeling systems examined 156–159; mental disorder language/thinking, moving from 160–161; summarizing 160
professional practices, alternative: assertive community treatment (ACT) 142–144; mindfulness teaching 103–104; spiritual approach 104–106, 135–138; symptom treatment and investigation 23; therapeutic community 133–135; voice-hearers, support strategies 139–141
professional practices, diagnostic: commercial impact of DSM 27; commercial sponsorship 59; 'diagnosis', illegitimacy and dangers 18–21, 27–29; DSM definitions as fraudulent 21–22; ODD assessment bias 47–50; political engagement 36–37; treatment, misuse of word 66
psychiatry, categories not diagnosis 18–20
psychotherapy: group 108–109; relational 106–107

Raeburn, Susan 108–109
Ragins, Mark 144–147
Rapley, Mark 140–141

Razzaque, Russell 103–104
Read, John 141
recovery model 144–147
relational psychotherapy 106–107
Robbins, Brent 6–7, 72–73
Roberts, Sande 112–113
Rogue & Rouge Foundation 130–132

school counseling 115–116
serious mental illness, alternative approaches: Gould Farm, therapeutic community 133–135; Hearing Voices Network 138–141, 148, 150; MHALA Village, recovery model 144–147; recovery-orientated 147–150; Spiritual Crisis Network 135–138; Thresholds, assertive community treatment (ACT) 141–144
Shannon, Scott 79–80
social therapy 109–111
Spiritual Crisis Network 135–138
spiritual psychiatry 104–106
'symptom picture' model 5, 35, 45, 63, 199–200

Thresholds, Chicago 141–144
Timimi, Sami 17–20, 83–84
transformational coaching 113–115
transpersonal psychology 136

United States (US): Artreach, Inc. 122–124; Creating Communities 124–128; Gould Farm, therapeutic community 133–135; It's About Childhood & Family, Inc. 117–119; juvenile bipolar disorder 63;

MHALA Village 144–147; Native Indians and ADHD label 38–39; Thresholds, Chicago 141–144

Walker, David 38–39
Walz, Chene 115–116

Wedge, Marilyn 39–40, 111
Weiner, Craig 7–8
Whitely, Martin 34–38

Yusim, Anna 104–106

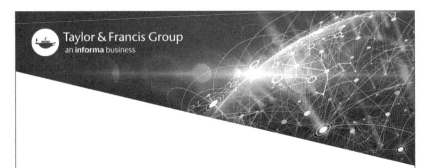